T0318172

Memos from a Theatre Lab

What does Immersive Theatre 'do'?

By contrasting two specific performances on the same theme – one an 'immersive' experience and the other a more conventional theatrical production – Nandita Dinesh explores the ways in which theatrical form impacts upon actors and audiences. An in-depth case study of her work *Pinjare* (*Cages*) sets out the 'hows' and 'whys' of her specific aesthetic framework.

Memos from a Theatre Lab places Dinesh's practical work within the context of existing analyses of Immersive Theatre, using this investigation to generate an underpinning theory of how Immersive Theatre works for its participants.

Nandita Dinesh teaches Theatre Arts and is Associate Director at the Bartos Institute for the Constructive Engagement of Conflict at the United World College, New Mexico.

Memos from a Theatre Lab

Exploring What Immersive
Theatre 'Does'

Nandita Dinesh

LONDON AND NEW YORK

First published 2017
by Routledge
2 Park Square, Milton Park, Abingdon, Oxon OX14 4RN

and by Routledge
605 Third Avenue, New York, NY 10017

First issued in paperback 2020

Routledge is an imprint of the Taylor & Francis Group, an informa business

British Library Cataloguing in Publication Data
A catalogue record for this book is available from the British
Library

Library of Congress Cataloging in Publication Data
A catalog record for this title has been requested

ISBN 13: 978-0-367-73657-6 (pbk)
ISBN 13: 978-1-138-21918-2 (hbk)

Typeset in Times New Roman
by Apex CoVantage, LLC

Contents

Introduction

Un Voyage Pas Comme Les Autres Sur Les Chemins De L'Exil (Chemins)

> The visitor is put into the situation so he or she can live the fear, the uprooting, the wandering, and the difficulties of acclimating to the receiving country.
>
> (Haedicke, 2002:102)

Spectator-participants to *Chemins* are asked to embody asylum seekers in the European Union (EU) through character profiles that are given to them at the beginning of the immersive experience. These character profiles document the narratives of real-life asylum seekers in the EU and with coloured stickers placed on their foreheads as crude markers of their race, spectator-participants are asked to undertake activities – like clearing immigration lines, folding laundry for extended periods of time, being attacked along the passageways of the performance space – in the shoes of the character allocated to them. For the duration of *Chemins* therefore, each spectator undertakes an individual journey as an asylum seeker to the EU.

I was first introduced to the idea of immersion through an article about *Chemins* in which Susan Haedicke (2002) describes her experience as an audience member who had to take on the role of an asylum seeker for this "*mise-en-situation*." Reading about *Chemins* sparked 'something' in my artistic explorations: the interest in a form that was completely novel to me; a form that expanded my understanding of audience participation; a form that, I thought, would fit very well within my work as a theatre practitioner-researcher in contexts of war. As a result I looked further into the creation of immersive environments like *This Is Camp X-Ray* (UHC Collective, 2013), explored the use of immersive training scenarios as part of the US military training regimen (Magelssen, 2009), investigated existing scholarship that surrounds how such performances/scenarios feed into the broad genre of Immersive Theatre, and participated in Immersive Theatre projects as an actor and a spectator. These different explorations finally informed the creation of a performance entitled *Pinjare (Cages)* that I created in collaboration with a theatre company in Kashmir. While I have analyzed *Cages* in other work (Dinesh, 2015a), the premise of this experience was to immerse male, Kashmiri audience members in the shoes of Kashmiri women, asking the spectator-participants to embody the gender-based differences in how the region's conflicts are experienced. *Cages* was conceptualized with the hope that the performance's use of a novel/unfamiliar aesthetic (in the context of Kashmir) might stand the chance of sparking new perspectives around age-old debates surrounding gender hierarchies. However, after the creation and implementation of *Cages*, there was one question that emerged for me: what does Immersive Theatre 'do' differently from 'conventional' theatre?[1] While I will more carefully delineate the differences between what I term as Immersive Theatre and as 'conventional' / 'traditional' / 'proscenium' theatre in Chapter 1, my approach to Immersive Theatre might be summarized for now as a form that creates a multi-sensorial, participatory aesthetic for its spectators; a script-centred performance that invites spectators to watch and listen being my understanding of 'conventional'.

Recent years have seen an increasing number of scholarly works about the wide genre of Immersive Theatre: debates about why 'immersion' might / might not be an appropriate concept to describe experiences like *Chemins*, analyses of the cognitive and pedagogical implications of different kinds of immersion, and articulations about the ethical conundrums that emerge from the use of a form that often leaves its spectators vulnerable and/or uncomfortable. Most recently Josephine Machon (2013) and Gareth White's (2013) books on *Immersive Theatres* and *Audience Participation in Theatre*, respectively, propose frameworks for the consideration of immersive aesthetics through theoretical analyses and through interviews with artists who use these forms. In addition to these two works that primarily address the experiences of spectators in immersive, theatrical environments, Leslie Hill and Helen Paris's (2014) *Performing Proximity* adds to this oeuvre by highlighting the perspectives of creators/performers in such intimate forms. However, while such existing scholarship articulates political, aesthetic, cognitive, and ethical questions that are embedded within immersive forms, my own queries around what Immersive Theatre 'does' are driven by the desire for an empirical, comparative study. In the context of existing analyses around Immersive Theatre therefore, and given my own practical explorations of this form, I often ask myself *why* and *how* the execution of an Immersive Theatre piece might differently impact spectators and actors in comparison to more 'conventional' theatrical performances.

In order to address this question, I place a qualitative research project at the centre of this book: a project in which two performances about the same theme were performed for, and by, creators and spectators from one College community in the United States. One of these performances was framed as an Immersive Theatre experience, and the other performance was created to be 'conventional' in its theatrical form. Each of these performances was followed by feedback mechanisms for both actors and spectators, and through an analysis of the data that emerged through these processes, this book generates theoretical propositions about what Immersive Theatre might 'do' differently from its more 'conventional' counterparts. Although I am aware of the challenges in attempting to evaluate what theatre 'does', I believe that understanding the *how* and the *why* behind my aesthetic choices is instrumental to my continuing work as an artist in places of war. For instance, when my colleagues in Kashmir ask me why they have to take on the roles of women in *Cages*, as compared to watching a play about women on a stage in front of them, I would like to be able to respond with a more nuanced answer than simply: "Well, because I prefer this aesthetic." Therefore, I went into this experiment hoping to explore the potentially different outcomes that might emerge from two distinct theatrical framings. That said, I certainly allowed for the possibility that the study would reveal nothing more or less than an aesthetic difference – that there actually might be no difference in what the two aesthetics 'did'; rather, simply a distinction in how such performances are created.

Since I keep referring to what Immersive Theatre 'does', it is important that I clarify how I understand the notion of 'impact' in the context of this project; a project that I will term as falling under the umbrella of Applied Theatre for its application within an educational setting and toward a learning-centred purpose (more on this in Chapter 1). While there have been attempts to study the impact of Applied Theatre initiatives in the context of HIV/AIDS-related work (Blakey & Pullen, 1991; Dunne, 1993; Elliott, 1996; Frankham & Stronach, 1990; Hillman et al., 1991; McEwan et al., 1991, to name a few), the approach of this experiment – exploring the impacts of two different aesthetic forms that address the same theme – is novel in what it seeks to do. Underscoring the potential importance of efforts to articulate what Applied Theatre does, Michael Etherton and Tim Prentki (2006:14) mention that "impact in applied theatre initiatives and projects might also encompass the wider political and economic results of the interventions of this work for individuals and communities." While the "immediate impact of a project of applied theatre may be measurable and may be included within" questions of measurement and evaluation, "there are also alterations in attitude and behaviour that are registered in the long term, sometimes over years and generations" (Etherton & Prentki, 2006:140) – and it is such (potentially) articulable medium and long-term alterations that particularly intrigue me. As Helen Nicholson comments (in Etherton & Prentki, 2006:143),

> for those of us engaged in research and dramatic practice which take place in community, educational and institutional settings, there is a need to submit our work to critical questioning as part of a continual process of negotiating and renegotiating our ethical positioning.

In this vein, I see the qualitative research in this project as being about a process of "theory building" rather than being about "testing or verifying theory" (Hughes & Wilson, 2004:71). Jenny Hughes and Karen Wilson (2004:71) say that research which generates theory "is an important but neglected area of evaluation in the participatory arts" where, often, "researchers are asked to provide 'hard' evidence of impacts (in the form of identification of measurable or verifiable outcomes)." Agreeing with these authors that "[m]easurements lack meaning unless aligned to a clear set of propositions about how the creative process 'works'" (Hughes & Wilson, 2004:71), this book seeks to offer theory-generating propositions about two particular aesthetic modes of engaging in Applied Theatre.

While the qualitative experiment in this project is novel within the realm of Theatre & Performance Studies, it must be noted that similar attempts have been made to assess immersive environments through other disciplinary lenses. For example, in literature surrounding simulation-based learning we see resonances between the characteristics of immersive scenarios like *Chemins* and the processes involved in the creation of a simulation. Simulations are described as including:

> (1) predefined learning goals and objectives; (2) a description of how the case will play out, including plans for appropriate responses from the simulator to the participants' actions; (3) scripts for actors who play the voice of the simulator [. . .] Included in the plan [is] a method for setting the stage for the exercise and creating a safe learning environment as part of the introduction.
>
> (Wang, 2011:668)

"Simulation learning is any learning that is deliberately contrived to appear real, and which relates to a real situation, but isn't in fact real" and there are said to be "degrees of simulation" that range "from simple role plays right through to disaster response training experience" (McAllister, Searl & Davis, 2013:1453). Simulations in the health education realm in particular are said to draw in conventions that are "seen in process drama and applied theatre" since "they are both concerned with affective and cognitive involvement" that involve "active learning processes and intentionally focus on exploring attitudes and values" (McAllister, Searl & Davis, 2013:1456). Speaking to the benefits of simulation-based learning in the medical and business contexts, it has been said that simulation could provide a "perfect opportunity for active experimentation by allowing the learner to try out new ideas immediately," thus fostering "active experimentation [that] promotes 'cementing' of new knowledge and long-term changes in practice" (Zigmont, Kappus & Sudikoff, 2011:50). In a similar vein, Laura Steck et al. (2011:264) discuss the benefits of students' participation in a simulation versus traditional (lecture-based) classroom environment by describing an assessment task that was structured around the creation of "an assignment in which students addressed the questions 'What?' 'So what?' and 'Now what?'" Steck et al.'s (2011:264–265) assignment

> directed students to record observations and reflections about the experience ("What?"); to generalize their observations and reflections in a broader context, noting how the experience does or does not confirm previously held assumptions ("So what?"); and to consider how their participation in the poverty simulation, and the subsequent knowledge and awareness acquired, may influence their attitudes and behaviors in future, real-life situations […] ('Now what?').

As a result of this study Steck et al. (2011:270) postulate that while assertions made "by an instructor regarding the structural inequalities and unique difficulties faced by those in poverty may fall flat or be perceived as naive or biased," using a simulation-based assignment "broke through defensive thinking on the part of many of our students."

The benefits of simulation-based learning seem to be echoed in much of the literature around this pedagogical approach. For instance, Zigmont, Kappus and Sudikoff (2011:49) argue that "[u]nlike lecture-based or teacher centered-learning, simulation requires learners to apply their current mental models [by providing] a great opportunity for individuals to control their learning to improve or refine their mental models." Furthermore, simulations might "provide concrete experiences during which learners can identify knowledge gaps upon which they can reflect" (Zigmont, Kappus & Sudikoff, 2011:50). Since the "most profound educational experiences are those that are emotionally charged, challenging, and stresses the learner," these researchers stress that well "designed simulations cause a significant change of body state to foster meaningful reflection, yet are not so stressful as to impede learning" (Zigmont, Kappus & Sudikoff, 2011:50). Additionally, in the medical education realm, the positive impact of simulation-based learning is "being described in terms of real patient outcomes" (Wang,

2011:666), and this pedagogy has been seen "to enhance student engagement, improve motivation to learn, and increase learning enjoyment" (Steck et al., 2011:261). "The literature also shows that simulation-based learning consistently decreases anxiety among novice nursing students at their first clinical experience" and "promotes their level of self-confidence and clinical competence" (Khalaila, 2014:253). Furthermore, simulation-based learning is also seen to raise "the students' satisfaction with learning" and to improve "their level of knowledge, and clinical performance" in addition to "their self-efficacy" (Khalaila, 2014:253).

All this being said, literature about simulation-based learning is careful to emphasize that more evidence is required to substantiate the notion "that simulation experiences improve 'real-world' actions and learning, not just at the end of the simulation experience, but also years later" (Gabrielsson, Tell & Diamanto, 2010:12). Such discussions reiterate the concerns espoused about Immersive Theatre where, echoing Haedicke's (2002) critical reflection around her willingness to participate in *Chemins* as a theatre aficionado compared to the reticence of some of her fellow spectators, it is documented that

> a common problem that is difficult to overcome in even the most well-executed simulation experiences, is that students may realize the setting is artificial and fail to fully engage, attend or remember. That is, students have not suspended their disbelief.
>
> (McAllister, Searl & Davis, 2013:1453)

In addition, it has been cautioned that "simply including simulation" is "not sufficient to guarantee learning" and the challenges have been articulated as "the potential for simulation learning to be 'intimidating' and even 'fearsome' for some learners"; as "the transferability of simulation learning to practice"; as "the difficulty in obtaining evidence of learning having taken place during simulation, given that such evidence would require the demonstration or observation of change in a learner's behaviour" (Berragan, 2014:1144). Despite these challenges, however, the increased use of simulation-based approaches in different contexts substantiates the hypothesis that something different happens in these immersive environments as compared to their less immersive counterparts; a 'something' that I seek to articulate within the use of Immersive Theatre simulations.

A particular example of simulation-based learning might also be seen in virtual reality (VR) exposure as a way to treat post-traumatic stress disorder (PTSD) for returning United States army personnel. "Strictly speaking, using virtual reality to treat combat-related P.T.S.D. is not new," and versions of such simulations were visible in 1997, when "researchers in

Atlanta unveiled Virtual Vietnam" (Halpern, 2008). "Ten combat veterans with long-term P.T.S.D. who had not responded to multiple interventions participated in a clinical trial of Virtual Vietnam," and all of them are said to have shown "significant signs of improvement, both directly after treatment and in a follow-up half a year later" (Halpern, 2008). Building on the principles of Virtual Vietnam, "Virtual Iraq is a tool for doing what's known as prolonged-exposure therapy, which is sometimes called immersion therapy"; an approach to "cognitive-behavioral therapy" that has been "derived from Pavlov's classic work with dogs" (Halpern, 2008). In addition to using virtual reality immersion to work with war vets, researchers such as Joann Difede have "treated victims of September 11th with a program called Virtual W.T.C." (Halpern, 2008). In these virtual simulations, Shih-Ching Yeh et al. (2009) say that "the visual stimuli presented in the VR Head-Mounted Display" are augmented by "directional 3D audio, vibrotactile and olfactory stimuli" that seek to recreate multi-sensorial environments akin to Immersive Theatre scenarios. Similar to the improvisation that is called upon from actors in Immersive Theatre environments who have to adapt their scripts in accordance with spectators' responses, the clinician's interface in VR-based simulation therapy provides a clinician "with the capacity to customize the therapy experience to the individual needs of the patient" (Yeh et al., 2009). Through the use of such interfaces therefore, the VR environment echoes the importance of multi-sensorial strategies in Immersive Theatre where "the patient can be placed by the clinician in VR scenario [in] locations that resemble the setting in which the trauma-relevant events occurred," modifying "ambient light and sound conditions" so as "to match the patients description of their experience" (Yeh et al., 2009). While researchers of VR-based exposure therapy are cautious in generalizing from existing trials, they do use "accepted diagnostic measures" to state that "80% of the treatment completers in this VRET sample showed both statistically and clinically meaningful reductions in PTSD, anxiety and depression symptoms, and [that] anecdotal evidence from patient reports suggested [. . .] improvements in their everyday life situations" (Yeh et al., 2009).

The aforementioned benefits of simulations and simulation-based learning also find resonance in principles surrounding active learning and experiential education, as White (2013) indicates in his book. While active learning is not always more useful or powerful than conventional didactic/lecture-based pedagogies, it has been suggested "that active learning techniques [are] more effective for achieving specific goals, such as application to real-world problems" (DeNeve & Heppner, 1997:232). Since action learning/experiential education differ "from traditional forms of teaching as it emphasizes learning-by-doing with work-related issues and problems" (Gabrielsson, Tell & Diamanto, 2010:3), "studies have shown that this is a highly effective way to learn, providing very high recall relative to more traditional forms of learning" (Brown, 2003:22). For example, Edgar Dale (in Brown, 2003:24) "argues that 'doing' is the best way to learn," supporting his argument "with research that shows that two months after training, learners will typically remember 20 per cent of what they *hear*, 30 per cent of what they *see*, 70 per cent of what they *say*; and 90 per cent of what they *do*" (emphasis in original). While active/experiential learning is not always guaranteed to evoke more powerful results, learning-by-doing becomes most effective when learning "begins with an impulse or experience;" followed by an "observation of the surrounding condition" that involves "reflecting on the experience and comparing it to prior experiences;" an observation that is heightened by knowledge "obtained partly from recollection and partly from the information, advice, and warning of those who have had a wider experience;" knowledge that is finally underscored by judgement that "combines observation and knowledge into an interpretation of the significance of the experience" and "translates the meaning of the experiences into the purpose – a desire to change or to create a plan of action for future similar experiences" (Wang, 2011:671). Donald Kirkpatrick (in Wang, 2011:676–677) offers another way to conceptualize the learning that occurs from doing and proposes that it "consists of four levels: Level 1 – reaction; Level 2 – learning; Level 3 – behavior; Level 4 – results," where each "level has an impact on the next level." While "Level 1 (reaction) measures participant satisfaction," the second level of learning "measures the extent to which learners change attitudes, improve knowledge and skills because of the training"; the third level of behaviour "measures the extent to which the training led to a change in behaviour," and "Level 4 (results) measures the bottom line impact of the training in the real world" (Wang, 2011:676–677).

These ideas from active learning and experiential education contain parallels with concepts from cognition and memory – a relationship that has been theorized by Bruce McConachie (2007, 2008; McConachie & Hart, 2006) who draws links between theatre and cognitive neuroscience. While such scholarly undertakings offer ways to think through the cognitive implications of spectatorship in the theatre, there are specific ideas that are relevant to this project. Of particular significance is the notion of "embodied action," where the term 'embodied' is seen as highlighting "the kinds of experience that come from having a body with various sensorimotor capacities" and that "these individual sensorimotor capacities are themselves embedded in a more encompassing biological, psychological, and cultural context" (Shapiro, 2011:52–53). As a result, to "say that cognition is embodied means that it arises from bodily interactions with the world" and as such, the cognition that occurs depends on "the kinds of experiences that come from having a body with particular perceptual and motor capabilities" (Shapiro, 2011:56).

In this vein, "[l]ooking at pictures of humans in painful situations also activates brain activity in the area that is active in the emotional appraisal of pain, but not the area that is active with the actual sensation of pain" (Di Benedetto, 2010:14). Therefore, the use of the physical body of the spectator in Immersive Theatre creates room for the hypothesis that different cognitive process might occur in a multi-sensorial, embodied spectatorship as compared to the dual, sensory spectatorship process of 'conventional' performance. So, although we have the "ability to activate the same neural areas in our own brains when we observe actions and emotions in others, we are aware of the differences between ourselves and others" (Di Benedetto, 2010:15), and each of the senses that are activated in our bodies affects the cognitive processes that are consequently triggered. Therefore, when multiple "senses are being directly triggered, we do not have time to doubt the skill or veracity of the aroma, the drip, or the jolt" and therefore, our "brains will experience the event as if we have lived through it" (Di Benedetto, 2010:103–104). By "activating all senses or senses that are beyond words or sight, we can break through the constraints and patterns offered by conventional theatrical invitations" (Di Benedetto, 2010:122). And thus, performances "that harness more than our eyes and ears to perceive the world encourage us to wake up, to be alert to the world around us, and to actively interact with the objects and creatures around us" (Di Benedetto, 2010:122), creating a different kind of memorial and cognitive experience.

The potentially distinct manifestations of cognition in multi-sensorial settings lead me to an exploration of memory vis-à-vis how immersive and non-immersive theatrical experiences are remembered and how often, or why, these memories are recalled. For instance, "authors specify that autobiographical memories are only those memories that are long lasting and centrally involve the self" (Davies & Wright, 2010:119), and because the spectators' self is construed differently in Immersive Theatre, do these experiences create different kinds of autobiographical memories? What mechanisms would allow for an insight into diverse constructions of the self in different approaches to spectatorship? Since it has been argued that "unconscious transference is particularly likely when two individuals are seen in close temporal and spatial proximity" (Davies & Wright, 2010:148), what happens when the spectator sees themselves in the shoes of another? The differences in how experiences are encoded in memory might be understood by Endel Tulving's (in Davies & Wright, 2010:211) classification of memory "on the basis of experience," in which it is proposed that "memory retrieval is either self-knowing or not and this judgement was something that only the participant in an experiment could report." "'Self-knowing' or 'autonoetic' memory describes a memory where the first-person experience was of 'remembering'" while memory "without self-knowledge, 'noetic', is often described as 'just knowing'" (Davies & Wright, 2010:211). Does this distinction between knowing and remembering become useful in understanding the difference between the two forms of spectatorship analyzed in this project – that one form of remembering a performance might be autonoetic, while the other might be noetic?

While the potentially beneficial implications of Immersive Theatre are acknowledged through the various perspectives that I described earlier, it is important that I also devote some discussion to the ethical challenges and risks of this aesthetic. Lyn Gardner (in Shaughnessy, 2012:192), for instance, articulates her concerns about the ethics, risks, and anxiety of such immersive forms as follows:

> Theatre is changing so rapidly that many of the old conventions are going out the window. There may not be any seats. You may not know quite where to stand. There may not be any other spectators – or, indeed, any actors. You may discover that you are the show, which raises questions about exactly who is taking the risk and who should be paying [. . .] The makers of immersive and interactive theatre experiences who are creating work that is exploring new ways of engaging with audiences are in completely new territory, both physically and mentally. They are going to have to find ways to create experiences for their audiences where risks can be taken without causing audience anxiety to rocket.

In addition to their potential for causing anxiety Diana Taylor (2009:1890) critiques the US Army's immersion techniques in which "planners do not involve members of the opposing side in the enactment," thus furthering the idea that "the enemy is always one of us – an extension of our fears and fantasies, which nonetheless have perilous implications for others." Jill Bennet (in Shaughnessy, 2012:6–7) furthers this assessment by emphasizing that the affects catalyzed by immersive/simulated experiences might ultimately manifest in a crude empathy in which "another's experience" is seen as being "assimilated to the self in the most simplistic and sentimental way," thus failing "to respect the difference between" the Other's experience and the spectator's own. Furthermore, such a

> conjunction of affect and critical awareness may be understood to constitute the basis of an empathy grounded not in affinity (feeling for another insofar as we can imagine being that other) but on a feeling for another that entails an encounter with something irreducible and different, often inaccessible.
>
> (Shaughnessy, 2012:6–7)

Immersive Theatre might thus be critiqued for creating environments that are "artificial, manufactured, consumerist product[s], reducing art to a series of cheap (or expensive) simulated thrills" (Shaughnessy, 2012:186). Yet another concern about Immersive Theatre lies in the power dynamics that are created between the performer and the spectator-participant in these aesthetics and rather than immersive performances necessarily engendering an atmosphere for spectators to be equal participants that co-create the work (as many immersive pieces claim to do), there is a valid concern that these performances might "require the spectator only to 'complete' the performance" because the show has already been scripted (Wozniak, 2015:330). Spectators themselves are aware of this dynamic, and in a study that was done after Contact Young Actors Company's production of *People in Glass Cases Shouldn't Throw Stones*, members of the audience expressed their concern that

> they could be in the way of other audience members or performers [. . .], that they might be "made to" participate in a physical way, that they were worried about interacting in the right way, that they were unsure "what was going on", and that partaking means taking responsibility for the performance.
>
> (Gröschel, 2015:361)

Questions surrounding the ethical dimensions to simulated experiences do not end there, and the poignancy of these dilemmas can be witnessed in Stanley Milgram's (1961; in Perry, 2013) obedience experiments and in the Stanford Prison Experiment (1971; in Zimbardo, 2007): two (in)famous instances in which simulated environments were created as studies in social psychology. While my intentions with the use of Immersive Theatre are certainly not comparable with the goals of a social psychologist, there is an undeniable component of studying human behaviour that becomes inevitable. However, while social psychologists might ask "[t]o what extent can an individual's actions be traced to factors outside the actor, to situational variables and environmental processes unique to a given setting?" (Zimbardo, 2007:8), the experiment in this project asks how an individual's *re*actions can be linked to aesthetic strategies that are unique to particular settings. The link between theatrics and simulated social psychology experiments has not gone unnoticed, and Milgram is said as describing in an unpublished interview (Perry, 2013:50):

> Setting up an experiment is much like producing a play; you have to get all the elements together before it is a running production [. . .] I can spend months perfecting the format of a document used in an

experiment; and I will not allow the experiment to proceed, until everything is not only adequate but aesthetically satisfying.

In this vein Gina Perry (2013:58) suggests that that Milgram "knew before his first subject arrived [. . .] what sort of results he wanted to achieve, and he had used pilot studies and pretests to hone the design to achieve just that." Understanding the place of theatrical aesthetics within this undertaking Perry (2013:282) suggests that Milgram "guessed that his experiments were more successful as drama than as science" and postulates that "Milgram's theatrical flair overtook his scientific objectivity." Similar observations have been made about the Stanford Prison Experiment, that the study "has as much intuition as strictly scientific method in its design [and] may have had the makings of a work of art" (Zimbardo, 2007:255). However, after some time in the simulated prison "a few prisoners, rather than simply seeing all this as annoying play that they can bear with for as long as it takes (at $40 a day), see it as a genuinely evil situation and quit the 'experiment' for good" (Zimbardo, 2007:255). In crafting this comparative experiment, therefore, I was quite aware that I would have to conceptually navigate the challenges that accompany the use of simulated environments in Immersive Theatre.

Before moving on to the conceptual framework, which describes my attempts to address these challenges, there is one last element that needs to be clarified, and that is the role that auto-ethnography plays in my writing about theatre; an approach that I have used extensively and varyingly in my writing thus far (Dinesh, 2014, 2015a, 2015b, 2015c, 2016). Auto-ethnography is always interwoven differently in each of my writing projects, and in this book, the use of this strategy manifests in *Memos from a Theatre Lab (Memos)* that begin and end each chapter. These *Memos* seek to contextualize the central discussions in each chapter with personal accounts of experiences that have informed this project, and since memoing "is the act of recording reflective notes about what the researcher [. . .] is learning from the data," the *Memos* in this book function as "records about concepts and their relationships" (Given, 2008:505), albeit in a personalized way. Given my belief that the personal and the subjective quality to theatre making needs to be foregrounded in attempts to use practice as research, the *Memos* in this book might be seen as my own process of record keeping via descriptive texts that seek both to complement the more analytical accounts that surround them and to document some of the 'intuitive' decisions and judgements that I made during this project. Ultimately, the *Memos* are a way of performing my voice; of occupying the worlds of practice and research; of being unable to disentangle myself from the biases that pervade how I interpret the data that emerges through this work.

Having used this introduction to explain the rationale behind this project, the potential and challenges of immersion as demonstrated by existing studies, and the place for auto-ethnography in this book, I move forward to the next chapter. Chapter 1 sets out the theoretical and conceptual frameworks that guide this project: how I define Immersive Theatre and 'conventional' theatre; how I approach the processes of data collection and analysis.

Note

1 I place 'conventional' in single quotation marks in this introduction until I further clarify the term in Chapter 1. Once my definition has been established I alternate between the terms conventional / traditional / proscenium (without quotation marks) to refer to the performance that is thus crafted.

Works cited

Berragan, L. 2014. Learning nursing through simulation: A case study approach towards an expansive model of learning. *Nurse Education Today*. 34:1143–1148.

Blakey, V. & Pullen, E. 1991. You don't have to say you love me: An evaluation of a drama-based sex education project for schools. *Health Education Journal*. 50:161–165.

Brown, Rupert. 2003. Just do it: Why simulation learning beats chalk and talk. *Simulation Learning*. 22–25.

Cages. 2013. Performance. Srinagar, Kashmir.

Davies, G. M. & Wright, D. B. 2010. *Current Issues in Applied Memory Research*. New York: Psychology Press.

DeNeve, K. M. & Heppner, M. J. 1997. Role play simulations: The assessment of an active learning technique and comparisons with traditional lectures. *Innovative Higher Education*. 21(3):231–246.

Di Benedetto, S. 2010. *The Provocation of the Senses in Contemporary Theatre*. New York: Routledge.

Dinesh, N. 2014. Solidarity and soldier(ity): Using theatre in military contexts. *activate*. 3(1):47–57.

Dinesh, N. 2015a. Delusions of singularity: Aesthetics, discomfort and bewilderment in Kashmir. *Research in Drama Education: The Journal of Applied Theatre and Performance*. 20(1):62–73.

Dinesh, N. 2015b. In-between spaces: Theatrical explorations from Rwanda to Kashmir. *South African Theatre Journal*. doi:10.1080/10137548.2015.1011857.

Dinesh, N. 2015c. Poetics and (mis)representation: Creating theatre with/for/about ex-militants in Kashmir. *Performance Research: A Journal of the Performing Arts*. 20(1):113–122.

Dinesh, N. 2016. *Theatre & War: Notes from the Field*. Cambridge: Open Book Open Book Publishers (full name of the publishing house).

Dunne, N. 1993. *Acting for Health Acting against HIV: A Report on the Effectiveness of Theatre in Health Education in HIV and AIDS Education*. Birmingham: Theatre in Health Education Trust.

Elliott, L.G.L. 1996. Theatre in AIDS education – a controlled study. *AIDS Care.* 8(3):321–341.

Etherton, M. & Prentki, T. 2006. Drama for change? Prove it! Impact assessment in applied theatre. *Research in Drama Education: The Journal of Applied Theatre and Performance.* 11(2):139–155.

Frankham, J. & Stronach, I. 1990. *Making a Drama Out of a Crisis: An Evaluation of the Norfolk Action against AIDS Health Education Play.* Norwich: University of East Anglia, Centre for Applied Research in Education.

Gabrielsson, J., Tell, J. & Politis, D. 2010. Business simulation exercises in small business management education: Using principles and ideas from action learning. *Action Learning: Research and Practice.* 7(1):3–16.

Given, L.M. (Ed.) 2008. *The Sage Encyclopedia of Qualitative Research Methods.* Thousand Oaks, CA: Sage.

Gröschel, U. 2015. Researching audiences through walking fieldwork. *Participations: Journal of Audience & Reception Studies.* 12(1):349–367.

Haedicke, S.C. 2002. The politics of participation: *Un Voyage Pas Comme Les Autres Sur Les Chemins De L'Exil. Theatre Topics.* 12(2):99–118.

Halpern, Sue. 2008. Virtual Iraq: Using simulation to help a new generation of traumatized veterans. *New Yorker.* Available: http://www.newyorker.com/reporting/2008/05/19/080519fa_fact_halpern?currentPage=all. [2015, November 12].

Hill, L. & Paris, H. 2014. *Performing Proximity: Curious Intimacies.* Basingstoke: Palgrave Macmillan.

Hillman, E. et al. 1991. Pregnancy, STDs and AIDS-prevention: Evaluation of new image teen theatre. *AIDS Education and Prevention.* 3:328–340.

Hughes, J. & Wilson, K. 2004. Playing a part: The impact of youth theatre on young people's personal and social development. *Research in Drama Education: The Journal of Applied Theatre and Performance.* 9(1):57–72.

Khalaila, R. 2014. Simulation in nursing education: An evaluation of students' outcomes at their first clinical practice combined with simulations. *Nurse Education Today.* 34:252–258.

Machon, J. 2013. *Immersive Theatres: Intimacy and Immediacy in Contemporary Performance.* Basingstoke: Palgrave Macmillan.

Magelssen, S. 2009. Rehearsing the "Warrior Ethos": "Theatre Immersion" and the simulation of theatres of war. *Drama Review.* 53(1):47–72.

McAllister, M., Searl, K.R. & Davis, S. 2013. Who is that masked educator? Deconstructing the teaching and learning processes of an innovative humanistic simulation technique. *Nurse Education Today.* 33:1453–1458.

McConachie, B. 2007. Falsifiable theories for theatre and performance studies. *Theatre Journal.* 59(4):553–577.

McConachie, B. 2008. *Engaging Audiences: A Cognitive Approach to Spectating in the Theatre.* Basingstoke and New York: Palgrave Macmillan.

McConachie, B. & Hart, E. 2006. *Performance and Cognition: Theatre Studies and the Cognitive Turn.* Oxon and New York: Routledge.

McEwan, R. et al. 1991. Drama on HIV and AIDS: An evaluation of a theatre in-education programme. *Health Education Journal.* 50:155–160.

Perry, G. 2013. *Behind the Shock Machine: The Untold Story of the Notorious Milgram Psychology Experiments.* New York and London: New Press.

Shapiro, L. 2011. *Embodied Cognition.* New York: Routledge.

Shaughnessy, N. 2012. *Applying Performance: Live Art, Socially Engaged Theatre and Affective Practice.* London: Palgrave Macmillan.

Steck, L. W., Engler, J. N., Ligon, M., Druen, P. B. & Cosgrove, E. 2011. Doing poverty: Learning outcomes among students participating in the community action poverty simulation program. *Teaching Sociology.* 39(3):259–273.

Taylor, D. 2009. Afterword: War play. *Modern Language Association of America.* 124(5):1886–1895.

UHC Collective. 2003. *This Is Camp X-Ray.* Performance. Manchester, UK.

Wang, E. E. 2011. Simulation and adult learning. *Disease-a-Month.* 57:664–678.

White, G. 2013. *Audience Participation in Theatre: Aesthetics of the Invitation.* Basingstoke: Palgrave Macmillan.

Wozniak, J. 2015. The value of being together? Audiences in Punchdrunk's *The Drowned Man. Participations: Journal of Audience & Reception Studies.* 12(1):318–332.

Yeh, S.-C., Newman, B., Liewer, M., Pair, J., Treskunov, A., Reger, G., Rothbaum, B., JoAnn Difede, J., Spitalnick, J., McLay, R., Parsons, T. & Rizzo, A. 2009. A virtual Iraq system for the treatment of combat-related posttraumatic stress disorder. *The Proceedings of the IEEE VR2009 Conference.*

Zigmont, J. J., Kappus, L. J. & Sudikoff, S. N. 2011. Theoretical foundations of learning through simulation. *Seminars in Perinatology: Simulation Center.* New Haven, CT: Yale University.

Zimbardo, P. 2007. *The Lucifer Effect: Understanding How Good People Turn Evil.* New York: Random House.

1   The framework

Memo #1

My first personal experience with Immersive Theatre was as a performer in a piece entitled *Fight or Flight* (2010), a piece that was inspired by the Red Cross' refugee simulation educational kit *In Exile for a While* (Red Cross, n.d.) and created by two Theatre Arts students at the College that I was teaching at in India at the time. In line with the Red Cross guide, the students' twelve-hour immersive piece was "meant to create mock feelings of intimidation, confusion, anger, disempowerment and hopelessness in the minds of the participants" through the use of threatening "border guards, rude camp employees, mistreatment of women and children, boring food, realistic props and unpleasant surprises" (Red Cross, n.d.:5). All of these strategies were employed in *Fight or Flight* to help spectator-participants "gain awareness of what real refugees may be feeling" (Red Cross, n.d.:5).

Fight or Flight was composed of around forty spectator-participants, all students between the ages of sixteen and nineteen, from different parts of the world. Similarly, the cast for the event was composed primarily of students, with a few faculty members (including myself) performing roles as needed by the student directors of the piece. With this composition of actors and audiences, *Fight or Flight* was structured as follows:[1] spectator-participants met at a central location on the College campus. The facilitators shared the game rules and distributed character profiles. Once the character profiles were distributed and the rules of the game were established, participants were divided into two groups: an Illegal Group (IG) and a Legal Group (LG) of refugees. Each group took a different path, encountering different circumstances en route. Eventually though, both the IG and the LG end up at a refugee camp where they 'rest' for the night. If at any point spectator-participants did not cooperate, the actors would call an intimidating rebel/guard to take the uncooperative spectator-participant to an isolation cell that was manned by my character. After a night of restless sleep in the camp, actors woke up the spectators, telling them that the situation has worsened and that everyone had to leave immediately. All the spectators arrive at the last location where they are served tea. The directors return to speak with the audience members and to let them know that the experience has ended. Spectator-participants are invited to come for a debriefing session later the same day.

Fight or Flight was my first experience as an actor in an Immersive Theatre performance, and the most important takeaway for me was around stereotyping. In particular, I left with many questions about the way in which the guards/rebel characters in the piece needed to behave – as being authoritative, intimidating, abusive – so as to maintain 'control' over a spectator-participant population that outnumbered the actors. For instance, when I was first asked to take on the role of the isolation cell guard, I was told by the directors to be "mean" and to use my own biases and prejudices about immigration officials to shape my character. Directed to dress in dark clothes, smoke cigarettes, and be intimidating, the co-directors of *Fight or Flight* also asked me to take on this role since the blending of a teacher (who already had a degree of power over student spectator-participants) with the character of an aggressive/powerful guard would more likely ensure the student spectator-participants' following the rules of the immersive environment. While crafting the characterization of the guard I tried to challenge my own stereotypes of immigration officials – having lived in many different contexts as an immigrant, I do not necessarily view these individuals in the most positive light. And yet, I had to wonder, should I really portray the guard in such a stereotypical way? Could there be other ways to show the guard's power? Or better still, was there a way to portray a 'good' guard who was caught up in the system and who tried, in his/her own way, to be helpful to the refugees s/he watched over? However, would this kind of characterization be possibly deemed as being inauthentic to a majority of refugee experiences in which 'good' guards might very well be an anomaly? With these questions in mind, during the first few hours of the performance I played a guard who was aggressive but also had elements of kindness and patience. About two hours into my performance, however, a fellow faculty-participant who had been watching my performance from afar came up to me and said: "You're just being yourself, Nandita. You need to be more intimidating. More guard-like. Otherwise, you're going to ruin the show." Embarrassed at being chastised by a colleague, my guard suddenly became a meaner person. She spat at the refugees. Swore more often. She even took one of the actor-refugees from the group outside the isolation cell (something that was completely improvised) and asked the actor to scream as though the guard was committing a violent act against her. . .

Being an actor in an Immersive Theatre event pointed me toward questions around the ethics of representation in such works. Is there a place for nuance when placing spectators in the shoes of an Other? Can we move away from stereotyping neither the experience of the 'victims' nor of the 'perpetrators'?

***

My second personal encounter with Immersive Theatre was in a piece entitled *Wonderland*. Inspired by Lewis Carroll's *Alice's Adventures in Wonderland* (1993) and *Through the Looking Glass* (1999), one of my other Theatre Arts students in India decided to create an immersive theatrical experience. *Wonderland*'s concept was centred on the idea that audience members would embody their own Alice – multiple Alices who would then explore *Wonderland* as best suited them.

Wonderland was designed to occur early in the morning, at dawn. Audience members were asked to arrive at a central location the night before the performance, and we were requested to spend the night in that space. This location, which was a large multi-purpose hall, was decorated with a number of clocks and mirrors and also included a wall with the projection of an optical illusion playing on a loop. The projection played over the course of the entire night until an actor playing the White Rabbit character from Lewis Carroll's book woke the spectator-participants at dawn. The White Rabbit then took the audience members (in groups) to *Wonderland*, where we encountered and interacted with different characters from the books. *Wonderland* occurred in an outdoor area on the College campus that had been landscaped to look like a maze – like a labyrinth. As the audience members walked around the maze, bleary-eyed from a night of optical illusions and white rabbits, we were invited to a tea party, were the victims of innumerable pranks, and were invited (implicitly) to become Alice. To make her *wonderland* our own.

I remember going to sleep that night looking at the optical illusion being screened in front of me. I also remember waking up multiple times over the course of that night, bewildered by the twirling lights and images that kept playing on the wall. On one of these midnight wake-ups, I think I saw someone dressed like a mad hatter. Did I, though? Disoriented, I went back to sleep only to wake up again, to see someone dressed like a rabbit waking up people around me. I couldn't go back to sleep after that. I wasn't entirely sure what was real and what wasn't – even though I had been privy to my student's idea from the get-go, I was disoriented in the way that only sleep deprivation can achieve. Although I was expecting to see characters from *Alice in Wonderland*, I hadn't imagined what it might feel like to see them through eyes brimming with sleep . . . Suddenly, the actor dressed as a White Rabbit woke me up and, discombobulated from a night of tossing and turning on a cold, hard, floor, I experienced *Wonderland* in a bit of a haze. The director had achieved what she wanted, I think. She had put me in a state of mind that made *Wonderland* seem more illusion-like; more on the borderline between dream and reality . . . Walking back home that morning, I couldn't help but wonder about how different the sensations that *Wonderland* provoked for me would have been had my student chosen to stage the performance as a proscenium piece.

***

My third personal encounter with Immersive Theatre lay in directing *Cages* as a collaborative, Immersive Theatre piece that was part of my doctoral work in Kashmir. Working with a theatre group in Srinagar, I designed a three-week workshop process that was structured around the five different senses – toward creating a piece that would both speak to some element of the conflicts in Kashmir, while placing spectators in the shoes of an Other. The theme and structure of *Cages* emerged through collaborative exercises and discussions during the workshop, and the decision to target *Cages* toward a specific audience of Kashmiri men – each show could only accommodate two spectators – was also a decision that was taken in collaboration with the artists that I was working with. Finally, through the experience of creating *Cages*, I was finally able to see Immersive Theatre through yet another perspective, the perspective of the director.

In this experience, I often revisited my experiences as an actor (*Fight or Flight*) and as a spectator-participant (*Wonderland*) to Immersive Theatre. I critically reflected upon the struggles that I had encountered as actor and spectator, and in so doing tried to address a couple of aspects: to carefully address how 'victims' and 'perpetrators' were portrayed as a result of my experience in *Fight or Flight*; to negotiate my spectator-participants' comfort/discomfort as a result of what I had experienced in *Wonderland*. In making these decisions, *Cages* answered some of the questions that emerged for me from *Fight or Flight* and *Wonderland*. However, the performances of *Cages* brought up new questions: questions around ethics; questions around the politics of using a form that made people powerless and vulnerable in a context that is already defined by powerlessness and vulnerability. Despite the pre- and post-performance discussions that I had designed to mitigate that vulnerability, spectator-participants to *Cages* were still powerless. And while the feminist in me was not entirely averse to placing male spectator-participants from a rigorously patriarchal context in an uncomfortable position, the ethics of that decision being made in an active conflict zone bothered me.

As a theatre researcher-practitioner who mostly works in contexts of conflict therefore, the vulnerability that I saw Immersive Theatre evoke for spectator-participants in a context like Kashmir made me go back to the drawing board. If I was going to ask my spectators to make themselves vulnerable to an experience like *Cages*, should I not be able to tell them *why* this approach might be more effective than a 'conventional' approach? If I want to use the Immersive Theatre aesthetic in times and places of conflict, should I not first attempt to understand the functioning of this aesthetic in contexts that are less volatile? *Cages* catalyzed me to think more carefully about the ethics of Immersive Theatre in places of war and in having to pay attention to the considerations that emerged, I started to design a comparative study about Immersive Theatre in a less contentious setting. Ultimately, I hoped that such a study would enable me to generate more nuanced insights into the use of Immersive Theatre in places of war.

Cages, Wonderland, and *Fight or Flight* have played an important role in my coming to the project in this book – an important role in shaping my questions about what Immersive Theatre 'does'.

Framing the aesthetics

Immersive Theatre is a hard-to-define genre, as Josephine Machon (2013:xvi) has indicated, "because *it is not one*. However, the use of immersion in performance does expose qualities, features and forms that enable us to know what 'it' is when we are experiencing it" (emphasis in original). Etymologically, the term immersive is said to have "developed from computing terminology, [and] describes that which provides information or stimulation for a number of senses, not only sight and sound" (Machon, 2013:21). At the heart of Immersive Theatre is the embodied experience of an event to which we are unlikely to have access in our everyday lives; an event during which, as Alan Kaprow says (in Machon, 2013:31), "the line between art and life" becomes "fluid, and perhaps indistinct, as possible." It is important to clarify at the outset though that I do not see Immersive Theatre as existing in a binary with a proscenium performance that engages the spectators' senses of sight and sound: Jacques Rancière (2010) among many others have already suggested that being an audience in a 'traditional' setting results in its own forms of immersion. That said, while I do see the term 'immersion' as being applicable in some way to all theatrical efforts, there are specific ways in which I use these aesthetics in the experiment described in this book.

First, I use the terms 'conventional', 'traditional', and 'proscenium' theatre to refer to pieces that are performed "by actors of scripted plays" and that take place "in front of audiences who are seated within buildings usually constructed for that purpose" (Pasquier, 2015:223). The audience does not verbally or physically interact with the actors; instead, they engage with the world of the performances only through their senses of sight and sound. On the contrary, what I term as Immersive Theatre places the notion of being 'participatory' at its core. In such participatory performances "the audience is able to affect material changes in the work in a way that goes beyond the inherent interactivity in all live performance" (Breel, 2015:369). Through this participation the spectators are offered "a level of agency [. . .] to creatively contribute to the work" and while "audience experience is central to all forms of live performance, it is a crucial aesthetic component of participatory work, as the responses and actions of the participants become part of the fabric of the show" (Breel, 2015:369). The term participatory is inherently broad, however, and includes

> interaction (where the work contains clearly defined moments for the audience to contribute within), participation (when the audience's participation is central to the work and determines the outcome of it), co-creation (when the audience are involved in creating some of the parameters of the artwork), and co-execution (where the audience help execute the work in the way the artist has envisioned).
>
> (Breel, 2015:369–370)

And because of this continuum on which we might place different degrees of participation in the theatre, I use the term 'immersive' to further qualify my particular application of a participatory aesthetic.

While it is easier for me to describe what I mean by a 'traditional' performance, my approach to an 'immersive' participatory aesthetic might be best presented through the presentation and discussion of three examples (see Table 1.1). In attempting to distil the particular characteristics with which I seek to infuse the immersive aesthetic in this project, however, I do *not* seek to propose a universal definition for *all* Immersive Theatre. Instead, by focusing on particular aesthetic characteristics of a certain approach to Immersive Theatre, this chapter presents a framework for the performance that will be created as part of this project.

Approaches to Immersive Theatre in works such as *Chemins, This Is Camp X-Ray*, and *Cages* resonate with Hans-Thies Lehman's (in Shaughnessy, 2012:12) concept of the "post dramatic" which encompasses a "shift from representation as the focus of dramatic enquiry to the relations between actor and audience." Nicola Shaughnessy links Lehman's thesis to Norman K. Denzin's (2003:24) call for a "turn to a performance-based approach to culture, politics and pedagogy," an aesthetic in which the traditional audience is said to disappear and instead become collaborators who "are co-constructed by the event" (Denzin, 2003:41). In their re-constructions, de-constructions, and co-constructions of spectators' identities pieces like *Chemins, This Is Camp X-Ray*, and *Cages* implement "scenarios," which Diana Taylor (2009:1888) puts forward as being "frameworks for thinking." Such frameworks might range from

Table 1.1 Three examples that frame my approach to Immersive Theatre

Example 1: Un Voyage Pas Comme Les Autres Sur Les Chemins De L'Exile (Chemins)	*Example 2: This Is Camp X-Ray*	*Example 3: Cages*
As described in the introduction.	*This Is Camp X-Ray* (UHC Collective, 2003) is the re-creation of a US government–controlled prison in Guantanamo Bay in a public Manchester building, creating two kinds of audiences. The first audience group includes a handful of individuals who volunteer to be spectator-participants and become prison inmates for a durational performance in which they live and are treated as prisoners for multiple days. The second audience group is composed of bystanders who pass by the installation every day, highlighting the way in which the Manchester residents (who are imprisoned in Guantanamo Bay) have become (in) visible in the public consciousness of their city.	*Cages* (2013) is a piece that I co-created with a theatre company in Kashmir in 2013. Two different actors usher in the two Kashmiri male spectators who attend each performance of *Cages*. "Where have you been, my sister?" an actor asks each audience member, "everyone is waiting for you. We must go inside." Immediately understanding that he has been given a character in the play, the audience member enters the building with the actor playing his brother and is taken into a room that represents his maternal home. The audience member is asked to wear bridal clothes – thus becoming a wo/man – and for the remainder of the performance lives in the shoes of (some) Kashmiri women. In this vein, the wo/man is asked to perform chores 'typical' to Kashmiri women: make tea, clean the home, and follow her in-laws' directives (Dinesh, 2015).

"theatrical as-if simulations of catastrophic events such as nuclear war to hypothetical what-if setups such as a ticking bomb to acts of torture" to scenarios "that aim to heal victims by working through trauma" (Taylor, 2009:1888). *Chemins* uses immigration interviews for asylum seekers at European Union (EU) nations' points of entry as one of its scenarios; the second example creates scenarios that are shaped by inmates' lives at Guantanamo Bay; *Cages* uses quotidian chores from the domestic lives of many Kashmiri women as scenarios for the male spectators to reflect upon their relative privilege in those spaces. The frameworks for thinking that are implemented in these three examples seek to recreate real-world sites/settings by providing "information or stimulation for a number of senses, not only sight and sound" (Machon, 2013:21). Furthermore, the scenarios in these three examples foster Helen Nicholson's (2005:24) notion of an embodied practice of performance that dislodges "fixed and uneven boundaries of 'self' and 'other,'" and the participants in the three examples that frame my approach to Immersive Theatre graft the identities of Others onto the spectator-participants' own bodies. In so doing, the pieces seek to transpose the archive of the Other onto the repertoire of the Self: a psychological and physical identification that is explicitly sought between the spectator and the Other s/he embodies.

In addition to including a focus on more than two senses, I am particularly interested in immersive environments that have a pedagogical focus, that is, where the creators intend to create a space in which the spectator-participants learn about a very specific socio-political issue or theme. For example, *Chemins* contains the goal of educating spectators about the experiences of asylum seekers in the EU, *This Is Camp X-Ray* seeks to sensitize spectators about the residents of Manchester who are still incarcerated in Guantanamo Bay, and *Cages* aims to immerse Kashmiri men in the experiences of women so as to enhance their perspectives of gender. Unlike immersive environments that are more difficult to articulate in terms of a particular learning-based purpose – the works of the UK-based theatre company Punchdrunk, for example, where immersive environments are created as an aesthetic framework to stage existing scripts – the kind of Immersive Theatre that I am interested in specifically seeks to be educational. Furthermore, in these works' efforts to function as pedagogical arenas, they are applied to non-mainstream theatrical settings: a warehouse-type structure for *Chemins*; an abandoned building for *This Is Camp X-Ray*; different rooms in a house for *Cages*. Thus, given the ways in which such kinds of Immersive Theatre are applied toward educational purposes and performed in non-mainstream locations, I consider my approach to immersion in this book as sharing resonances with ideas from

Applied Theatre and Theatre in Education, though it is the former that I am most influenced by.

In addition to a learning-centred intention, the pedagogical underpinnings to my use of Immersive Theatre in this project are also highlighted in terms of the context in which I chose to execute it – a College that I work at in the United States. My co-creators and audience members were from a residential, educational institution in New Mexico, where I live and work. This College comprises a student body of around 250 students who come from over sixty countries; the students are engaged in the International Baccalaureate (IB) Diploma Programme (DP), are between sixteen and nineteen years of age, and comprise of two cohorts – first-year students and second-year students. In addition to the students, the College community includes both teaching and non-teaching staff that hail from a number of different geographical and cultural contexts. The co-creators and spectators for this project were recruited from this specific educational community through open invitations that are sent to students, teaching, and non-teaching staff.

While I could have chosen to implement this project in different contexts in which I am engaged, both within and outside New Mexico, there are a number of reasons that guided this choice of co-creators and audience members. First, the College in New Mexico is one among fourteen schools that are part of a larger network/movement that I have been personally involved with since the year 2000, first as a student and then as an educator in three of the fourteen institutions (India, Armenia, and now, the United States). Given the long-standing relationship that I have with this movement, therefore, there is a trust that is afforded me when I work with students and staff in this context, a trust that presents me with the benefits of being both inside and outside the community that I am working with. In terms of this project, for instance, I was an insider because of my relationship with this movement of Colleges and an outsider because I was new to this particular College community in New Mexico, having been there only since July 2015. Being simultaneously positioned as insider and outsider therefore allowed me a unique position from which to conduct this practice-as-research undertaking. Second, given that my co-creators, spectators, and I are all part of an educational community that uses English as its primary language of communication, the linguistic hurdles that have arisen in my Applied Theatre work in non-English speaking contexts were mitigated. For example, in Kashmir, despite being able to speak Hindi/Urdu, I find it very difficult to speak about theoretical ideas from Performance Studies in those languages. Having been academically educated and trained, for better or for worse, in English, this remains the language in which I am best able to communicate nuance. Therefore, I chose to work with an English-speaking participant group so as to eliminate the potential hurdle of mis-translations and mis-communications. Third, in addition to my positioning and the possibility of working in a common language, I chose this particular college community as my participant group for this project since my being part of the same community allowed for both formal and informal exchanges to occur, creating opportunities for collaborators and spectators to approach me about their responses in an unstructured way. Finally, given the context of being in an educational environment, I believed that my intentions with this research project were less likely to be seen as suspect or disingenuous by my co-creators and spectators. As has been articulated in many Applied Theatre initiatives, there is a conflict that often arises between the theatre practitioner-researcher's intangible goals and the collaborating population's desire for concrete outcomes as a result of that theatrical intervention. Working within this College presented more possibilities for the researcher and participants to be on the same page, that is, that the research itself could be a legitimate outcome; that outcomes that occurred beyond the generation of new knowledge might not necessarily be a point of contention.

The outcomes of my exploration of Applied Theatre in this project are not informed by a desire to cause measurable change or to define how spectators' learning should be channelled. I clarify this point since, for example, Applied Theatre projects in the public health arena often seek to catalyze behavioural changes among spectators so as to evoke specific health-based outcomes: asking audiences to use condoms so as to reduce HIV/AIDS rates in a particular community, for instance. In comparison, the three Immersive Theatre examples that frame this chapter do not have a tangible/specific behavioural outcome that they seek to evoke among their spectator-participants. Spectators to *Chemins* are not told how to use their newfound knowledge to assist asylum seekers in the EU; participants in *This Is Camp X-Ray* are not told which human rights groups they could join to protest against the continued incarceration of Manchester residents in Guantanamo Bay; the men who visit *Cages* are not told how to treat the women in their lives as a result of their immersive experience. Susan Haedicke puts forth a useful framework with which to consider such intangible outcomes by drawing from Ruth Frankenberg and Lata Mani (in Haedicke, 2002:283) and distinguishes between "decisive" shifts and "definitive" shifts. This distinction enables a differentiation between real changes in thinking and action (decisive shifts) and "a complete rupture in social, economic, and political relations and forms of knowledge [definitive shifts]" (Haedicke, 2002:283). As Haedicke (2002:115) says about the decisive shifts that she herself experienced as a spectator-participant to *Chemins*,

> As I reflect on my experience, however, I ask myself if and how I have really changed. Will I switch careers to fight for the rights of refugees?

Will I donate time to ease their plight? Will I do more than put money in the box by the cash register for refugees from Rwanda or Kosovo or Afghanistan or wherever the next conflict forces its citizens into exile? Probably not. And yet . . . I am transformed. Wanmin is still with me. Her identity and mine have merged, and I see her/my face when I hear stories about refugees. I look at issues of immigration with different eyes.

The approach that I take in this project vis-à-vis Applied Theatre, therefore, is geared toward decisive rather than definitive shifts.

In considering the factors that influence such decisive shifts *Chemins, This Is Camp X-Ray*, and *Cages* also invite a consideration of time and durationality. While *Chemins* and *Cages* do not incorporate durationality as an aesthetic element – in that the performances last for a 'conventional' one-hour time frame – *This Is Camp X-Ray* gives particular importance to time. Spectator-participants who take on the role of prison inmates in *Camp X-Ray* are asked to immerse themselves in the theatrical prison for a period of days. Furthermore, the second spectator group – of audience members who do not participate in the prison explicitly but witness the prison every day as they make their way around the city of Manchester – also sees the manufactured prison environment over the duration of the installation. Similarly, the importance of time in how immersive experiences are retained might be seen in the use of theatre immersion in the US Army training scenarios that are described in the introduction to this book. Given that the soldiers are expected to demonstrate definitive shifts in their behaviour in Iraq and Afghanistan as a result of their training environments, their immersive experiences are designed to occur over a period of days. Examples such as these force me to consider if/how the duration of a spectator-participant's immersive engagement might affect the ways in which the theatrical experience stays with them. That said, although time is an important variable to consider in assessing the afterlife of an Immersive Theatre performance, for the purposes of the experiment in this project durationality was *not* utilized as an aesthetic tool. This is to say that the two performances that are created as part of the experiment, the immersive and conventional pieces, were both crafted to last for the same amount of time. I made this choice so as to eliminate time as a mitigating factor in the responses and by creating a set of controls with which to compare the two aesthetic approaches – the controls being that the two performances would speak to the same theme, last for the same amount of time, and work with the same co-creator and spectator demographic – I hoped to be able to generate more reliable propositions about how Immersive Theatre works.

In addition to time, the notion of space might also be said to impact the causation of decisive shifts through Immersive Theatre. While proscenium theatre generally involves a set design within a demarcated physical space that is separated from the zones in which spectators are situated (i.e., the stage versus the seats in an auditorium), in Immersive Theatre experiences spaces are constructed and re-constructed so as to create a version, a 'sense', of the original site. For example, the creators of *This Is Camp X-Ray* (re)designed an existing building in the city of Manchester to look, both externally and internally, like the prison complex in Guantanamo Bay. In *Chemins*, "[c]urtains or temporary walls formed all of the many spaces" that the spectator-participants visited on their journeys (Haedicke, 2002:99). "The entire warehouse-like structure had been transformed into a veritable maze of narrow hallways, small and smoky bureaucratic offices, streets and shops of an unnamed town, a prison" – all locations that an asylum seeker to the EU might have to negotiate "on the road to exile" (Haedicke, 2002:99–100). Space played an important role in *Cages* as well, and we utilized the premises of the Kashmiri theatre company that I was collaborating with as the space for the performance. *Cages* was staged in the smaller rooms of the building – rooms that usually served as bedrooms, offices, and the kitchen – and this choice of space bolstered the subtext of the piece: the intention to highlight quotidian conflicts in the private spaces of people's homes, amid the larger, more public narratives of war. Mike Pearson (2010:8) says that a "variety of terms have stemmed from the term site-specific performance including 'site-determined', 'site-referenced', 'site-conscious', 'site-responsive', 'context-specific' ." Pearson (2010:7) further states that "the term refers to a staging and performance conceived on the basis of a place in the real world (ergo outside an established theatre)" and the creation of a performance in "this found space throws new light on it," fostering new and unpredictable relationships between the space and the performers/spectators who interact with it. Immersive Theatre experiments (like those that frame my approach in this project) might therefore be said to have been conceived with a real-world site in mind; consequently designing a theatrical, immersive world in which new light is shed on that space – thus creating more avenues for decisive shifts to occur.

Given the preceding discussion, Immersive Theatre in this project is composed of the following characteristics: (1) catalyzing decisive shifts in relation to a particular socio-political issue; (2) inviting spectator-participants to physically embody an Other; (3) provoking multiple senses, in addition to sight and sound, through a focus on how spaces are configured and designed. The performance that I term as being conventional shares some elements with its Immersive Theatre counterpart, particularly in the first characteristic of adopting strategies from Applied Theatre to catalyze decisive shifts among spectators. However, the differences manifest in the second and third characteristics, that is, in how spectators are involved in the performance and in the senses that are provoked through a configuration of the spatial component. Spectators in the immersive performance are spectator-participants who have a multi-sensorial experience; audience members to the proscenium performance are spectators who have a dual-sensory (sight- and sound-based) experience. Otherwise the two performances address the same theme, last for the same duration, and work with the same intention of catalyzing decisive shifts for its spectators.

Framing the experiment

The larger research methodology that has been employed in this project might best be termed as "inquiry as bricolage," where a "complex, dense, reflexive collage-like creation" is created to represent "the researcher's images, understandings and interpretations of the world or phenomenon under analysis" (Given, 2008:65). In this vein, this experiment invokes forms of inquiry and analysis that draw from "diverse theoretical and methodological resources in a manner that has more in common with art and literature than with natural science" (Given, 2008:65). In the most obvious sense this experiment might be described as a form of performance ethnography in its desire to describe and analyze spectators' responses to "products of intentionally created theatrical type performances" (Given, 2008:609). However, this work cannot only be viewed through the lenses of performance ethnography since its conceptualization and design draw from a variety of disciplines – from Performance Studies, Education, and Social Psychology, to name the disciplines that were drawn from in speaking to simulations, active learning, and virtual reality exposure therapy in the introductory chapter of this book. Since theoretical pluralism is said to occur "whenever qualitative researchers draw on more than a single theory as a theoretical framework to guide decisions about the research design and to make sense of their research findings" (Given, 2008:633), the methodological approach in this project certainly overlaps with paradigms other than those of performance ethnography.

Before describing the design of this theoretically pluralistic project, there are two clarifications that I would like to make. The first is that while qualitative research of this nature often gives rise to the question of how much data is enough data, I am in agreement with the likes of Norman K. Denzin and Daniel Miller who "suggest that one [. . .] interview may be 'enough' for case studies in qualitative research" (in Gomme, 2015:285; emphasis in original). I reiterate here that the goal in this project is "not an abstract, or empirical generalization"; instead, the objective is "concerned with providing analyses that meet the criteria of unique adequacy" where each analysis is "fitted to the case at hand" and the data is "studied to provide an analysis uniquely adequate for that particular phenomenon" (Gomme, 2015:285). This has been termed as a "method of instances" where "each instance of a phenomenon, for example an interview [is taken] as an occurrence which evidences the operation of a set of cultural understandings currently available for use by cultural members" (Gomme, 2015:285). In this approach whether or not "the particular utterance occurs again is irrelevant" (Gomme, 2015:285); what is analyzed is precisely that which did/did not occur within the instance under examination. In addition to a method of instances approach, the second clarification to make is that while I am primarily interested in the responses of spectators to the two performances, I agree with Rachel Gomme's (2015:286) concern that "the majority of critical writing on one-to-one performance comes from the point of view of the spectator and considers intimacy as experienced on only one side of the equation." Performers' accounts are few and far between, and Leslie Hill and Helen Paris's recent work (2014) is one of the few exceptions that speaks to performers' experiences of intimately interacting with their spectators. Sharing Gomme's concern, I decided in the midst of the rehearsal process that the actors in each performance would also function as spectators to the other performance (i.e., the performance that they did not perform in); that actors would also participate in feedback sessions similar to those designed for spectators. As such the immersive and proscenium performance each had two groups of spectators: one group that was composed of actors from the other performance and a second group of spectators who only saw one of the performances. Therefore, while this project was initially conceptualized to only consider feedback from spectators, in the spirit of emergent design, the data collection methods were later adapted to also include the performers, toward creating a more holistic understanding of what Immersive Theatre 'does'.

Both performers and spectators who participated in this project were recruited via open, emailed invitations that were sent out to the entire community of students and staff at the College. The first round of invitations sought co-creators and outlined the project in general terms: the time commitment that would be required and the fact that this project was part of a larger research effort. Further details about the comparative nature of the experiment were shared only when a group of performers was finalized – a choice that I made so as to not give away too much information about the experiment to the same community that would later be invited as spectators to the performances. Later, once I had a committed group of performers, I held a general information session during which the actors were informed about the utilization of different aesthetic strategies in the two performances and the comparative goals of the research project. However, the performers were *not* informed about the specific differences between the two aesthetics; the performers were also *not* informed about the methods and strategies that would be used in the post-performance phases of data collection. Furthermore, specific requests for confidentiality were made to the performers, so as to reduce the likelihood that members from the potential pool of spectators would have prior knowledge about what the experiment sought to understand. Once the performances were ready, similar to the process of recruiting co-creators, spectators were invited to the performances (via email) and the information that was shared in the invitation simply stated the following: the two possible times and venues at which the performances might be experienced, the limit on the number of audience members that could be accommodated at each showing, and that spectators to the performances would need to commit to attending feedback sessions.

While I chose to work with the College population in New Mexico for the reasons outlined earlier, I believe it would also be accurate to describe my respondents as forming a "convenience sample" (Given, 2008:67) of sorts. Since a "convenience sample can be defined as a sample in which research participants are selected based on their ease of availability," the actors and spectators were "individuals who [were] the most ready, willing, and able to participate in the study" (Given, 2008:124). By working with this convenience sample from the College, data was collected after the performances by using questionnaires, group discussions, one-to-one interviews, and diaries: questionnaires and group discussions took place a day after the performance, and at this session diaries were given to all spectators and actors to make entries over a one-month period. One month after the performances, actors and spectators were invited to individual post-performance interviews, at which time the diaries were also collected from them (the specific design of each of these instruments is explained in the discussion that follows). Finally, in addition to these instruments, I allowed for the possibility that unstructured/unpredictable interactions might occur with individual spectators and co-creators on the College campus.

The questionnaires

Table 1.2 presents the questions that were designed for the next-day questionnaires alongside indications of the concepts that each question hoped to assess. Every query drew inspiration from a particular concept that I encountered while researching simulation-based learning, virtual reality exposure therapy, active/experiential education, and existing analyses of Immersive Theatre. Furthermore, rather than being about their potential to reveal certainties, the questions were designed to unearth concepts that would be useful in generating theoretical propositions to benefit my work with Immersive Theatre in places of war. And finally, since the questions were created in relation to performances that are two different adaptations of Kay Adshead's (2001) *The Bogus Woman*, it is necessary to mention that the shows' premise deals with the global refugee crises that were/are taking place across the world. More information about the two performances will be provided in the next chapter.

Table 1.2 Questionnaires for the spectators and actors

Questions for actors and spectators	Designed to understand the similarities/differences in
What, according to you, were the main themes of the performance? *Actors were asked this question for both performances, the one they acted in and the one that they watched.*	General interpretation of content and form
What, according to you, were the intentions of the creators, i.e., what were they intending to evoke from the audience? *Actors were asked this question for both performances, the one they acted in and the one that they watched.*	
What is one element from the play – a scene, a technique, a character – that you found most powerful? Why? *Actors were asked this question for both performances, the one they acted in and the one that they watched.*	Aesthetic judgements and preferences
For spectators to the immersive performance: In the role you were given during the performance, did you believe your story to be true? Why/Why not? *For spectators to the proscenium performance:* Do you believe the story of the protagonist? Why/why not? *Actors were asked this question for both performances, the one they acted in and the one that they watched, about whether or not they believed the story of the central character.*	Critical distance/intellectual judgement of content
As a result of this play, which of the following statements best describes how you have been affected (You can circle more than one response): • I am better informed about the experiences of refugees and asylum seekers • I encountered an interesting story • I want to help refugees and asylum seekers • Other: *Actors were asked this question for both performances, the one they acted in and the one that they*	Short-term outcomes

Rank the statements below from ***most to least relevant*** in the blanks provided. The statement that is most relevant to the performance you watched should be ranked 1 and the statement that is least relevant should be ranked 4:

- Empathy for refugees is what is most important in addressing the current global refugee crisis
  _____
- Activism for refugees' rights is what is most important in addressing the current global refugee crisis _____
- Information about refugees' situations is what is most important in addressing the current global refugee crisis _____
- Immigration policy reform is what is most important in addressing the current global refugee crisis _____

Actors were asked this question for both performances, the one they acted in and the one that they watched.

Real-world applications

Which character in the performance did you most identify with, i.e., which character said/did something to remind you of a personal memory? Please describe what the character said/did. If you did not identify with any particular character, please leave this section blank.

Actors were asked if there was something about the character they played that they did/did not identify with.

Identification

Space for additional comments or thoughts (if any)

Additional comments/concerns that were not addressed in the earlier questions

The group discussion and individual interviews

The group discussions and individual interviews were semi-structured: I provided participants with prompts and questions in order to guide the conversation; however, the spectators and the actors had control over the specific items that were discussed. In the group discussions in particular, the participants were invited to start the conversation by asking a question that they wanted to hear their peers' perspectives on – the intention being my desire to comprehend the specific elements that each different group would want to discuss. In comparison, the individual interviews were more structured since there were particular topics that I wanted to ensure were discussed: what the spectators remembered about the performance, what the actors remembered about the rehearsal process and the performance, and how the participants found the process of keeping diaries. However, while I began the individual interviews with these questions, here too the participants were welcomed to extend the conversation with their own questions or comments.

The diaries

I decided to use diaries since, in addition to using the entries to facilitate a content analysis of post-performance memories, I wanted to allow for the possibility that the frequency of entries might also provide evidence as to which group of spectators was more 'affected' by their performance. This is to say, do spectators from the proscenium piece make more/fewer entries in their diaries than their peers who experienced the immersive performance? If there emerged a significant difference between the average numbers of entries in each group, what reasons could be attributed to this occurrence? And if there emerged no difference in the frequency of entries, what other indicators might diary entries contain? Although diaries are not always reliable and "may be deliberately falsified" (Gunter, 2000:97), I ultimately decided that this data collection instrument would present more advantages than challenges in allowing for an individualized way of collating spectators' responses. Individual notebooks were provided to each of the spectators and actors when they attended the group discussion the day after the performance with this note pasted on the front page of the journal:

> *Please make notes in the journal as and when you recall the performance over the next month. If you can, please note the following:*
>
> •   *The date on which you make the entry*
> •   *The stimulus that made you recall the performance*
> •   *The specific aspect of the performance that you remembered*
> •   *The thoughts and/or emotions evoked by the memory of the performance.*

The questions above are simply prompts to guide your entries. Please feel free to craft your own questions or write in an unstructured fashion – whatever works best for you! The journal will need to be handed in when you come to your interview in one month.

With these data collection mechanisms presented, it is also essential that I speak to the ways in which data was analyzed in this project. Before doing that, though, I must admit that there are two inherent limitations to my processes of analysis. The first limitation is that I assumed, in all the data collection processes, that the participants meant what they said. Furthermore, I assumed that the respondents' use of specific terms (like empathy, for instance) meant what I understood them to mean. While the national diversity of the actors and spectators makes this a huge assumption, especially when we add to the mix that English was not the first language for many of respondents, my reasoning behind this assumption was the cultural homogeneity of the College community. In my experience within this particular movement of Colleges over the last fifteen years, I have found its students and staff to use a certain 'standardization' in their use of the English language despite varied backgrounds and linguistic capabilities. Therefore, when analyzing the responses in this project, I did not overly problematize *how* the words were used; rather, I looked only at *what* was said and accepted the responses at face value. The second limitation that I would like to highlight in my data analysis is that despite the small sample size (more on the exact numbers in the following chapter), there was a relatively large amount of data that was generated. While I have attempted to be as clear as possible in the following chapters, in explaining why I have decided to focus on specific pieces of data rather than others, it cannot be denied that there might an element of (unintentional) bias in how the data has been analyzed and discussed.

With these limitations in mind, the data that was collected using diaries, interviews, discussions, and questionnaires was analyzed through the use of induction in an exploratory data analysis framework. Content analysis was applied toward the material that emerged and "[r]ather than beginning with a theory, an explanation, or an interpretation and then seeking evidence to confirm, disconfirm, or otherwise test it in a deductive mode," the data analysis in this project was shaped by inductive thinking (Given, 2008:15). I began with the evidence, that is, "the particular," and attempted to excavate "theories, explanations, and interpretations to reflect or represent those particulars" (Given, 2008:15). Furthermore, since "[c]lassification is another central feature of analytic induction" (Given, 2008:15), the collected data was analyzed so as to generate different systems of categorization. The categories were developed inductively, and I approached the "data analysis without a preset list of categories" (Given, 2008:71). I developed

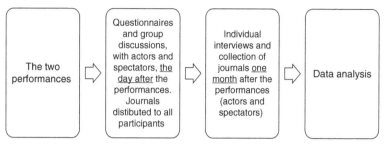

Figure 1.1 Experiment Design

a coding frame from the data, and this coding frame subsequently influenced the shaping of material from the interviews, discussions, diaries, and unstructured interactions "into instances, examples, and illustrations that ultimately make up the storyline summarizing the data (explanation of phenomena)" (Given, 2008:71).

Ultimately therefore, the project was therefore designed as follows (see Figure 1.1 above).

Memo #2

Before moving on to a discussion about the creation of the performances, it is important to clarify that I did not seek to find a simplistic answer as to whether or not an immersive aesthetic might be 'more' or 'less' affective/effective than its proscenium counterpart. Rather, the objectives of this experiment were intricately intertwined with my own goals as theatre practitioner/ scholar in times and places of conflict, where I remain intent on using immersive forms of theatre making. While I realize that there might be no need for my having to 'justify' why I prefer a form like Immersive Theatre or my approach to it – it is my artistic inclination and that's all the justification there might need to be – it is the ethical questions that arise from using immersive forms of theatre in contexts of war that make it relevant for me to grasp, more carefully, the quandaries that my aesthetic choices might/might not be mired in. And since conducting such experiments in active zones of conflict come with varied risks, it was more feasible to execute this research in my far more controlled

College lab – using what emerged in the lab to then reflect back into my theatre work in places of war.

Therefore it is important to underscore the fact that while my identity as a theatre educator in formal educational settings shapes how I approach this project, the questions I ask about Immersive Theatre are ultimately geared toward understanding how insights from this experiment might apply to my work outside formal classroom settings, in conflict zones. It is this goal that ultimately shapes how I analyze the data that emerges and it is entirely possible that looking at the same data through a different lens might reveal other dimensions. Before moving on to a description of the creative processes, data collection, and analyses then, it is important that the reader clearly understands my priority with this experiment: to tie in what I learned through this endeavour with the use of a piece like *Cages* in a conflict zone like Kashmir.

Note

1 The notes about the structure of *Fight or Flight* are taken from emails and documents that were shared with me, as a cast member, by the two student directors of the piece.

Works cited

Adshead, Kay. 2001. *The Bogus Woman.* London: Oberon Books.

Breel, A. 2015. Audience agency in participatory performance: A methodology for examining aesthetic experience. *Participations: Journal of Audience and Reception Studies.* 12(1):368–387.

Cages. 2013. Performance. Srinagar, Kashmir.

Carroll, Lewis. (1865) 1993. *Alice's Adventures in Wonderland.* London: Macmillan. Reprint, New York: Dover.

Carroll, Lewis. (1871) 1999. *Through the Looking Glass.* London: Macmillan. Reprint, New York: Dover.

Denzin, N. K. 2003. *Performance Ethnography: The Call to Performance.* Thousand Oaks, CA: Sage.

Dinesh, N. 2015. Delusions of singularity: Aesthetics, discomfort and bewilderment in Kashmir. *Research in Drama Education: The Journal of Applied Theatre and Performance.* 20(1):62–73.

Fight or Flight. 2010. Performance. Pune, India.

Given, L. M. (Ed.) 2008. *The Sage Encyclopedia of Qualitative Research Methods.* Thousand Oaks, CA: Sage.

Gomme, R. 2015. Not-so-close encounters: Searching for intimacy in one-to-one performance. *Participations: Journal of Audience and Reception Studies.* 12(1):281–300.

Gunter, B. 2000. *Media Research Methods: Measuring Audiences, Reactions and Impact.* London: Sage.

Haedicke, S. C. 2002. The politics of participation: *Un Voyage Pas Comme Les Autres Sur Les Chemins De L'Exil. Theatre Topics.* 12(2):99–118.

Hill, L. & Paris, H. 2014. *Performing Proximity: Curious Intimacies.* Basingstoke: Palgrave Macmillan.

Machon, J. 2013. *Immersive Theatres: Intimacy and Immediacy in Contemporary Performance.* Basingstoke: Palgrave Macmillan.

Nicholson, H. 2005. *Applied Drama the Gift of Theatre.* New York: Palgrave Macmillan.

Pasquier, D. 2015. The cacophony of failure: Being an audience in a traditional theatre. *Participations: The Journal of Audience & Reception Studies.* 12(1):222–233.

Pearson, M. 2010. *Site-Specific Performance.* Basingstoke: Palgrave Macmillan.

Rancière, J. 2010. *Dissensus: On Politics and Aesthetics.* London: A&C Black.

Red Cross. n.d. *In Exile for a While: A Refugee's Experience for Canadian Youth.* Ottawa: Canadian Red Cross.

Shaughnessy, N. 2012. *Applying Performance: Live Art, Socially Engaged Theatre and Affective Practice.* London: Palgrave Macmillan.

Taylor, D. 2009. Afterword: War play. *Modern Language Association of America.* 124(5):1886–1895.

UHC Collective. 2003. *This Is Camp X-Ray.* Performance. Manchester, UK.

2 The two performances

Memo #3

Directing one performance at a time is difficult enough, but trying to devote equal amounts of time and energy to the creative process of two different performances was a new challenge for me. The primary challenge, as someone who has a strong aesthetic affinity for Immersive Theatre, lay in ensuring that I would not, however inadvertently, make one piece 'stronger' than the other. Going into the process of creating two performances then involved a new kind of discipline in my way of working: where every choice that I made in one piece was placed in conversation with the manifestation of that strategy in the other performance. Making sure that the characterization was done in a similar fashion. Making sure that the scripts were making the 'same points'. Making sure that both performances also honoured the original text.

As I briefly mentioned in the previous chapter, this project's performances dealt with the themes of immigration/seeking refuge/asylum in a country that is not one's own. What I have not mentioned yet is that the creation of these two performances also (ironically) coincided with my own immigration process to the United States; a process that took over a year to resolve itself; a process that cost me financially, emotionally, and politically.

I recall walking into the biometrics office where I had to get my fingerprints and photograph taken – despite having done this on multiple occasions for the previous visas that I have held to the same country. As I walked through the door the guard called out: "Please sanitize your hands before entering the waiting area" and pointed toward a bottle of hand sanitizer that was placed on a table near the entrance. I stopped. I must have done a double take. Was he asking me to sanitize my hands because of the colour of my skin? Before I could decide on whether or not to say something, the guard said something like "Everyone needs to do this. This is a USCIS regulation." Like that made it all better. But I had to sanitize my hands. I needed the visa. Didn't I?

I had to go to a doctor to get screened for various diseases as part of my visa application. I had to assure the immigration authorities that they were getting a clean and vaccinated foreign body into their country. That I was not diseased by the heritage of my 'third world' origins. This might sound a bit melodramatic, but there's no denying the poignancy of the ways in which one's body is policed during the immigration process – even when one is not seeking asylum or refuge, but making an application to immigrate simply because one's spouse is a national of that country. The doctor checked me out and while filling out the forms, told me in a slightly lowered voice "You know, this part of the United States, it's like being in a developing country." I was amazed at the ease with which the condescension flowed off her tongue, without the slightest consciousness that I was someone from this developing world that she spoke of so patronizingly. Someone who is proud of where I come from, despite being aware of the complexities that exist in my 'home'. The doctor didn't see that though. She just saw an immigrant who must be keen to leave her 'developing world' home for something better.

Almost a year after I began the process, I got my final visa interview. "Congratulations. I think you have married in good faith," we were told. I'm glad the immigration official felt well informed enough to make that judgement.

Choosing 'immigration' as the theme for the performances in this project, therefore, was not only because the topic was particularly relevant for the College community (more on this later). Choosing the broad realm of immigration as the theme for the performances in this project was also relevant to my own experience at that moment in time. An occurrence that made the process of the creating these performances simultaneously personal and academic.

When exploring why adults learn, it has been pointed out that adults "engage in learning largely in response to pressures they feel from current life problems" (Knowles, 1967:278). Therefore, the "basis for effective simulation-based training" has been said to reside in "adult learner-centered educational principles" (Wang, 2011:667): that learners "need to know why they need to learn something before undertaking the effort to learn it"; that adult learners "have a self-concept biased toward independent and self directed learning"; that adult learners value learning that is more "life-centered (also referred to as problem-centered or task-centered) [. . .] than subject-centered"; that adult learners will be "more motivated to learn by internal drives than external ones" (Wang, 2011:670–671). Therefore, when deciding on a central piece that would be adapted in two different ways for this experiment, I wanted to make sure that the topic would be relevant to my young adult actors and spectators. As such, given that the global refugee crisis was often a point of discussion in a College that both strives to make its students conscious of the world's socio-political realities and has students from refugee backgrounds, working with the theme of the refugee crisis seemed to be the most appropriate choice for the Applied Theatre performances that lay at the heart of this experiment. While I had initially considered using devised theatre processes as a means of generating material for the two performances, I quickly realized that this approach would add one more degree of unpredictability to the experiment. Since my approach to devised theatre is heavily centred on participant contributions, using this methodology could have meant that the two performances would not only have had different aesthetics, but also different content. Based on the particular contributions of the immersive and proscenium actors, who would have been working in two different devised theatre workshop groups, such an occurrence contained the likelihood of leading to extensive ramifications on the processes of data collection and analysis. Therefore, in order to add one more degree of 'control' to the experiment and to ensure that it was the same exact content that was being delivered in two different ways, I decided to work with an existing script and to adapt that text into an immersive version and a proscenium version. This choice thus implied that actors would only be involved in the staging of the pieces and not in the generation of material for them.

Once this decision was made, when I began investigating contemporary plays that dealt with themes around refugees or asylum seekers and that would relatively be accessible to the student performers (many of whom had never done theatre before), Kay Adshead's (2001) *The Bogus Woman* came to my attention. A script that is written for a solo performer in free verse, Adshead's text is centred on the character of a young asylum seeker in the United Kingdom (UK) who arrives in the country from an unnamed African nation. The Young Woman, as the protagonist is referred to, gives voice to her various encounters with immigration officials, fellow asylum seekers, lawyers, and other variously intentioned people in her sojourn through the UK's immigration system. Shuttled from the airport to different detention centres, to being granted temporary asylum outside contexts of incarceration, Adshead's *The Bogus Woman* culminates with the Young Woman's request for asylum being denied by the UK authorities and with her ultimate deportation to a home country, where she meets with a violent death. Through a series of soliloquies in which the Young Woman engages with the audience, and through a sequence of conversations that she has with the other characters (that she herself impersonates), Adshead's protagonist flits between past and present. We understand through the text that this Young Woman is a persecuted journalist in her home country; that she has lost many members of her family to violence; that she has been subjected to extensive physical violence as a consequence of which she has lost a child. Adshead's protagonist is faced with struggles at every turn and although the audience understands, through flashbacks, that the threats are real, this is not information that the UK immigration officials are privy to. Hence, the government denying her asylum. Hence, the Young Woman's final deportation. Hence, her death. The necessary permissions for this experiment's adaptations of *The Bogus Woman* were sought from Adshead and her agent – both of whom were encouraging and supportive of the undertaking.

Before going into descriptions of each of the adaptations of *The Bogus Woman* that were created in this experiment, though, it is necessary to mention a few other framing details. At the time at which the scripts were first adapted, I had to work with an estimate of the numbers of volunteers that would sign up for the project. Based on what I knew about the College community, I estimated that I would have a team of about twenty performers. As mentioned in the previous chapter, actors for both performances were recruited via emails in which students and staff at the College were asked to express an interest in participating as performers, and ultimately, there were about twenty-five volunteers who signed up. The initial email requesting volunteers did not say anything more than that the project involved a theatre experiment and the twenty-five students who expressed interest were then invited to a general informational meeting in which they were told of the premise of the project: that we would be creating and performing two performances about the same theme, using two different aesthetic forms. More information on the two forms was *not* disclosed, however, and the actors only knew the shape that their own performances would take. Furthermore, at this initial information meeting, actors were assigned to the two groups (immersive and proscenium) based both on their schedules and on the number of performers that I needed for each adaptation – I wanted a minimum of twelve performers for the immersive piece and exactly five performers for the proscenium version. In sharing their schedules, the actors automatically divided themselves into particular groupings: those who had busier schedules went into the immersive performance ensemble since each scenario in that performance was scheduled to meet only once a week, with the option for one extra rehearsal each week. The performers in the proscenium piece needed to be students who had time in their schedules to meet twice a week, for longer periods of time, and have the option of being present for one extra rehearsal each week. This difference in scheduling was conceived with the understanding that the immersive performance would require different rehearsal techniques, which would require independent work on the part of the performers. However, the aesthetics of the proscenium piece were seen as requiring more in-person rehearsals due to its script-based focus and its technical requirements. Finally, in addition to informing/ confirming rehearsal groups and schedules during the first meeting, actors were asked to sign a consent form that explicitly requested them to refrain from discussing their work with performers in the other performance and with their peers who were not part of the project. Given the closed nature of the community at the College, it was probable that word would spread quickly and hence the question of confidentiality was one that was stressed strongly. I did not want future spectators to come to the performances with prior knowledge of what they expected to encounter, thus increasing the likelihood for pre-determined responses being shared during the feedback mechanisms. Finally, with this basic framework established, the rehearsals began: they lasted for six weeks and the performances were held at the end of that time period.

Framing the performances

In my attempts to ensure that both the adaptations of *The Bogus Woman* would be controlled in the ways that I needed them to be there were a few choices that I had to make vis-à-vis the scripts. First, I decided to make the pieces 'context-less', in that all references to the UK were removed as were references to the Young Woman's home being somewhere in Africa.

The reasoning behind this choice was that while in the proscenium piece audiences might be more readily able to suspend their disbelief and forgive inconsistencies in accents and such, this was a suspension of disbelief that I could not assume would happen in the immersive adaptation. Since the audience members themselves were going to be asked to embody the asylum seeker in the immersive performance (the Immersive Theatre performance's character equivalent of the Young Woman), it seemed to me that mentioning a specific country or region of origin might make it all the more difficult, and potentially alienating, for the spectators to place themselves in the shoes of that character. Ultimately, by making it so that the context could be anywhere in the world I thought that audience members would encounter more ways of identifying with the story of the asylum seeker that they embodied. In addition to this change in how the context was invoked (or not) in my adaptations of Adshead's original script, the second shift lay in my decision to change how the performances ended. In the original script Adshead's Young Woman returns to her home country, and through the usage of gunshot shots and a monologue from the character of the Lawyer, we understand that the protagonist has been killed upon her return. Once again I realized that this kind of ending would be impossible to work with in an Immersive Theatre format since the audience members were being placed in the protagonist's role. How could we (with any degree of realism and without potentially traumatizing/completely alienating the spectator-participant) convey the notion of a violent return? In light of this concern then, both pieces were designed to end with the rejection of the protagonist's asylum application, leaving the 'what happens after' to the audience's imagination.

The immersive version

In the immersive adaptation of *The Bogus Woman*, when the audience members came in, they are seated in a waiting room that is under the supervision of two actors playing Waiting Room Guards. Each spectator is assigned a number and after the spectators have been waiting for about five minutes, a Lawyer walks in and calls out a number – the spectator who has been allocated that number is asked to identify himself or herself. The Lawyer then takes that particular audience member into a room, a space that becomes that spectator's space for the duration of the performance and functions as an interrogation room. Each audience member is assigned one Interrogator, one Lawyer, and one Fellow Detainee and whenever the audience members are given a chance to respond in the script, their responses are invited but never forced. The audience members' responses are also *not* integral to the development of the script. So, if the spectators did not ever choose to interact with the actors, the performers would carry on as scripted. Similarly, if the audience member responded with something, the actors were asked to take a pause – respond to the comment verbally or non-verbally, based on how equipped they felt to address the response – and move forward with the script.

In each respective interrogation room, the Lawyer begins by giving the audience member something formal to wear: a coat or a tie, for instance, to assist them with a more tangible transformation into their character of the asylum seeker/refugee. The spectator is briefed by the Lawyer as to why s/he is in the interrogation room and is prepared for the questions to come from an Interrogator. "If you ever you feel like you don't know the answer, please just look at me and I will do my best to answer on your behalf. Yes?" the Lawyer says, before exiting the room to fetch the Interrogator. After leaving the audience member alone in the interrogation room for a few minutes, the Lawyer and Interrogator return and the audience member is asked a series of questions (by the Interrogator) that take from Adshead's original script. Questions like: "You realize you have committed an offence entering the country with a false passport?," "You still claim not to know which organization the 'soldiers' came from specifically?," and "Did all four men rape you?" Some of these questions were designed to include a pause after the Interrogator posed them, which allowed the audience member a chance to respond. Other questions were designed for the Lawyer to respond to, on behalf of their client. The interrogation ends with the Interrogator saying, "Ok, this is where you will have to wait until we decide how to proceed," after which s/he and the Lawyer exit.

The audience member is once again left in the room, to wait alone, till the Fellow Detainee character is brought in by the Interrogator and left in the room with the audience member. This character tries to make the room feel more comfortable for both the audience member and themselves by: spraying perfume/air freshener to make the space smell less like disinfectant or hand sanitizer; sharing food that they have in their bag with the audience member; talking about their character's personal experience with the immigration system in this unknown country. Each of these choices was designed both to enable a connection between the spectator-participant and the Fellow Detainee, and to invoke the different senses of the audience members. Ultimately, the Interrogator re-enters and forcibly takes the Fellow Detainee away – since their asylum status has been denied – giving the audience member a glimpse into what will happen to them if their application is also rejected. When the Interrogator has taken the Fellow Detainee away, the Lawyer re-enters and, in the last part of the scene, says, "I am very sorry to have to tell you that your appeal has been dismissed by the Special Adjudicator. You'll have to go back home immediately." The audience member is then escorted to the exit of the building by the Interrogator and asked to go to the refugee assistance centre down the road (the Interrogator points vaguely in some direction to tell them where the centre is). The Interrogator then heads back into the building and the audience member is left at the doorstep. Meanwhile, the Lawyer goes back to the waiting area, calls the next number, and takes the next audience member through up to the interrogation room and the whole experience commences again.

There were eighteen actors playing six different sets of Lawyers, Fellow Detainees, and Interrogators and twelve audience members in the immersive performance, that is, each trio of the Fellow Detainee, Lawyer, and Interrogator dealt with two audience members. While the first six audience members were taken to their interrogation rooms therefore, the remaining six spectators had to sit in the Waiting Room – under the supervision of two other actors playing the Waiting Room Guards – until the first six spectators finished their respective journeys through the experience (See Figure 2.1). The six spectators who went through the experience in the second round had to stay for between thirty and forty-five minutes in the waiting room, based on how long the previous audience member took in navigating the experience: some actors spoke very quickly, others spoke more slowly; some audience members interacted a lot with the performers, others did not: reasons that contributed to how long each particular audience member's experience lasted. While waiting for their turn, the second group of six spectators had nothing to do: their phones were confiscated by the guards upon their entry into the space, and all they had to entertain themselves with was the projected video of very long infomercial about a particular brand of cooking equipment (a choice that was informed by what I had had to experience in immigration waiting areas myself). Furthermore, the Waiting Room Guards were scripted to have a coffee and doughnut break while these audience members waited, so as to increase the spectators' awareness of how long they had been in there.

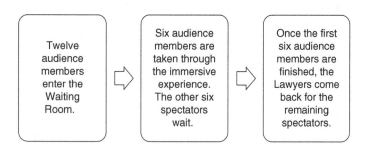

Figure 2.1 Sequence of events in the immersive adaptation

In addition to what occurred during the performance itself, audience members in this immersive adaptation were sent an application form a day before the show, and were asked to bring a completed copy of the form to the performance with them (see Figure 2.2). When the spectators entered the performance therefore, they had to present their completed forms and undertake a painstaking process with one of the Guards who would ask them to fill out a new form either if she identified an error in their existing

APPLICANT REGISTRATION FORM
దరఖాస్తుఉదరారయ నమోదదయ రయఖం

Please bring a printed copy of this form for your appointment at the Old Stone Hotel in Montezuma, New Mexico.

మోంటుజెజయిమరొ ఓల్డ్ స్టుటోన్ హోటెలో, న్యాయా మనెక్సీసీకో వదో్ద ఫనీబో్రవంది 27 న మరీ అపరాయరింటుామేండౖ కోసం ఈ రయూపం ఒక మయిద్రరితి తరీసయికయినవి దయచెనసీ, 1130 గంటలయ.

1. **Given Name** / ఇచర్చరీన పరేరయ: _____

2. **Family Name** / కయటయింబ పరేరయ: _____

3. **Home Address** / ఇంటుి చరీరయినవామ: _____

4. **Occupation** / వృతర్తిత: <u>Journalist</u> _____

5. **Reason for applying to immigrate** / ఇమర్మరిగర్రదేషన్ కరొ్సం దరఖాస్తుయ కరారణం:
<u>Seeking asylum due to dangers faced in my home country</u>

6. **Please read the following and sign below:**
దయచరేసరి కరింద చదవండరి మరరియయి కర్రరంది ఇనర్ చరేయండరి:

- • I understand that a lawyer will be appointed for me by the Department of Immigration.
  నరేనయ ఒక న్యయరాయవరొరదరి ఇమర్మరిగర్రదేషన్ కర్రఖి ద్వరారరా నరాకయ నరియామరించబడతరారయ అనవరి అరేధం.

- • I swear, at risk of perjury, that all the information stated on this form is accurate to the extent of my knowledge.
  నరేనయ అసతెయ పర్రమరాదం, పర్రమరాణ ఈ రయూపం లరో పర్రకటురించెరాదయ అనరనరి సమరాచరారం నరా జ్ఞర్రన మరేరకయ సమయిచరీతమర్లెనదవరి.

- • I agree to follow the rules and regulations set out by the Department of Immigration during my immigration interview.
  నరొ ఇమర్మరిగర్రదేషన్ ఇంటురర్ఫ్యయయాలరో ఇమర్మరిగర్రదేషన్ కర్రఖి ద్వరారరా ఏర్పరాటయ నరియామర్రలయ మరరియయి నరిబందనలయ అనయసరరించెండరి ఆంగరీకరరించినదరి.

I understand that not following these rules could lead to immediate expulsion, deportation, or arrest.
నరేనయ ఈ నరియామర్రలయ పరరాటురించకవరవటం తక్షణ బహరిష్కరణ, దరేత బహరిష్కరారం, లరేదరా అరెసర్టుట్ దరారరి తరరియావచ్చయ అనవరి అరేధం.

Applicant's name / దరఖాస్తుఉదరారయ యరార్కర్క పరేరయ: _____

Applicant's signature / దరఖాస్తుఉదరారయ యరార్కర్క సంతకం: _____

Date / తరీదరి: _____

ఈ రయూపం చరేయడం ద్వరారరా, దరఖాస్తుఉదరారయ భవరిష్యఉతర్తయలరో అరేజర్రిలయ మరరియయి అనయువరతనవరాటులరో ఉపయరోగరావవరికరి ఇంటురెలర్జరెనెస్ ఎజరెనెవరపరనర్ రరీకర్రయిడయలలరో ఉంచవరిన చరారరి సమరాచరారం ఆంగరీకరరించవరీందరి

Figure 2.2 Application form for spectators to the immersive performance

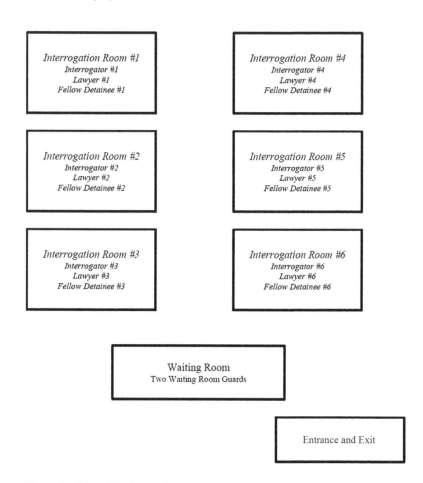

Figure 2.3 Map of the immersive space

forms or if the spectator had not brought the document with them. The forms were a way in which I sought to give the audience members an insight into the character that they would be given during the immersive experience – thus enabling them to be just a little bit less confused and vulnerable when they were asked to take on the role of the asylum seeker in the immersive adaptation.

The immersive performance took place in an academic building on the College campus, which had many narrow corridors and smaller classrooms. Six classrooms were designed to look like interrogation rooms while one of the larger rooms was designed to be the waiting area (See Figure 2.3). The corridors in the building were also pasted with different kinds of signs and posters, so as to ensure the maintenance of the immigration office environment should more perceptive members of the audience pay attention to the notice boards along the hallways, where different academic departments posted subject-specific information. The posters included messages such as: "Our immigration policies strive to encourage creativity. Here you can read poetry from a Creative Writing Workshop provided for children of refugees and asylum seekers. Join us. Find your voice," "Our offices serve over 5,000 people a day," "You are in good hands!," "We believe in diversity," "We believe in inclusion," "Aliens are allowed on these premises *only* if accompanied by a state appointed lawyer," "Our website receives more than 10,000 asylum applications a day," "You are welcome here," "We approve 5,000 asylum applications a month," "We are recipients of the 2015 *Excellence in Service* award for our work with refugees and asylum seekers," "We believe in free and fair trials for refugees and asylum seekers," "You are one step away from a better life," and "Deportation & Detention Quarters." Through this simple strategy, I hoped to be able to – in some small way – alienate the audience from a building that they were otherwise extremely familiar with.

As a final point about the immersive performance's creation, it is necessary to speak to the rehearsal process. The rehearsals for the immersive performance took place in seven different groups until the last two weeks before the performance – the six teams of Lawyers, Interrogators, and Fellow Detainees and the seventh group, which comprised the two Waiting Room guards. The rehearsal process began with table readings before moving on to characterization and blocking; I used two particular exercises that actors mentioned as being particularly beneficial to them in the crafting of their roles. The first was a character questionnaire, which asked the immersive performers to answer the questions in Table 2.1.

Using these questions each Fellow Detainee, Interrogator, Lawyer, and Waiting Room Guard crafted their own approach to their character. So, if one Interrogator defined his character as a "nice guy" (as one actor said) who behaved kindly and respectfully, that performer was given the space to edit his lines so as to reflect that personality trait. For instance, this Interrogator would sometimes say, "Look I really want to believe you, but . . ." instead of the scripted "I think your story is nothing but a pack of well-schemed lies." This Interrogator still, ultimately, rejected the spectator-asylum seeker's application, but did so in a more gentle fashion than some of his counterparts. Through this exercise the six immigration scenarios became slightly different from each other, although the premise remained exactly the same in each one.

Table 2.1 Character questionnaires (immersive adaptation)

FELLOW DETAINEES	INTERROGATORS	LAWYERS	WAITING ROOM GUARDS
How and why did you come to the new country?	What made you become an immigration official?	What made you become an immigration lawyer?	What is your name and what made you become a guard?
What are your aspirations for yourself, for your life in your new country?	What are your aspirations for yourself, in terms of your career?	What are your aspirations for yourself, in terms of your career?	Do you share information about your personal life with your colleagues? If yes, what kind of personal information do your colleagues know about you? If no, why don't you share personal information with your colleagues?
How and where did you meet your husband/wife? Describe your first date.	Do you want to believe the audience members' (refugees') stories about their experiences in their home country? If yes, why do you want to believe them? If no, why do you not want to believe them?	Do you believe your client (the audience member/ refugee)? Why/ Why not?	
How would you describe your attitude toward the refugee (audience member) who is being detained with you?		How do you feel when you have to inform the audience member (refugee) that his/her asylum application has been rejected?	What are your aspirations for yourself, in terms of your career?
What is likely to happen to you when you go back to your home country?	How do you feel when you have to reject the audience member (refugee)'s asylum application?	Outside the context of your job, how do you treat immigrants/ refugees that you might see in your neighbourhood or community?	How do you feel toward the refugees who come to your waiting room every day?
	Outside the context of your job, how do you treat immigrants/ refugees that you might see in your neighbourhood or community?		Outside the context of your job, how do you treat immigrants/ refugees that you might see in your neighbourhood or community?

The second exercise that worked well for the immersive performance's actors, once the actors were more familiar with their characters and once the blocking was settled on, was the creation of an 'if/then' matrix (as in Table 2.2). While I began the matrix for the actors with my own

Table 2.2 If/then matrix

If the audience member. . . .	Possible response
Says something inappropriate in response to your line	• Repeat your previous line • Stare at them and move on to the next line • If you feel comfortable improvising a line in your character, go ahead!
Gets impatient and says they want to leave	Say something like "You realize that if you leave, we cannot guarantee another appointment soon?" If they still say that they want to leave, the Guard should walk them to the exit. If the Guard is not in the room, the Lawyer or Fellow Detainee will knock on the door, call the Guard, and ask the Guard to walk the audience member to the exit. The Lawyer can go to the waiting room and get the next audience member.
Starts to cry or seems to be getting too affected	Say something like "I can see that you are not prepared for the interview at this time. Please reschedule your appointment." The Guard should walk them to the exit. If the Guard is not in the room, the Lawyer or Fellow Detainee will knock on the door, call the Guard, and ask them to walk the audience member to the exit. The Lawyer can go to the waiting room and get the next audience member.
Needs to use the bathroom	The Guard needs to escort them to the bathroom. So, the Lawyer or Fellow Detainee (if the Guard is not present in the room) will need to knock on the door and inform the Guard that the audience member needs to use the restroom.

Create your own combinations before the performance

suggestions, actors were welcomed to both edit my suggested responses and think through other possibilities to add to the list.

While each of the seven smaller groups within the immersive performance rehearsed separately for a month, in the last two weeks of the rehearsal process, all twenty actors rehearsed as an ensemble. Before the final shows, since the actors had only been rehearsing with me/each other until that point, we had one trial rehearsal with six invited faculty and students so that the performers might gain some experience at responding to different audience reactions. The second performance was for an audience group that included the five actors from the proscenium adaptation who came in as spectators to the immersive piece. The final audience group was composed of the twelve spectators, from the community at large, who signed up for the immersive adaptation.

The proscenium version

The proscenium adaptation went through more versions than the immersive performance, having to constantly adapt itself both to better suit the skill levels of amateur actors and to make it the same duration as the immersive piece. While Adshead's original is crafted as a solo performance, since I was working with many first-time actors, I decided from the outset that I would have to envision the performance so as to include multiple actors. As a result, I initially undertook an analysis of the various 'types' of characters in *The Bogus Woman* and based on what I interpreted the first version of the proscenium script divided the existing text among five actors: the Young Woman was always played by the same actor; Actor A played any character that represented the state; Actor B played any character in the text who was from the Young Woman's past and also those characters who were unhelpful in her present; Actor C played all the fellow detainee and refugee characters in the script; Actor D played the characters of those individuals who were helpful to the Young Woman in her new country.

While this categorized approach seemed to work successfully at first, I realized two weeks into the rehearsal process that the proscenium actors were having an extremely difficult task taking on multiple characters. Between the challenges of learning their lines and working on a nuanced characterization for the different roles that had been assigned within each character 'type', continuing in this vein seemed like it would result in a significant difference in acting quality between the immersive and proscenium performances. The immersive actors were progressing much more quickly than their proscenium counterparts since they only had one character to explore and fewer lines to learn – a task that seemed further simplified since the immersive performers' lines could be approached in the spirit of 'structured improvisation', where actors could change elements of what they said based on the audience members' responses and their individual characterization. Also, in addition to addressing a potential difference in the quality of the acting (which would no doubt affect audience responses), I realized that my first adaptation of the proscenium performance lasted twice as long as its immersive counterpart. As a result, since I wanted the length of both performances to be the same, I had to revisit my initial adaptation of Adshead's text and adapt it even further. The second (and final) version, therefore, contained a script that was even more streamlined and included a character allocation as follows: the Young Woman; Actor A played the Immigration Official; Actor B played the Detention Centre Guard; Actor C played the Fellow Detainee; Actor D played the Lawyer.

The twelve audience members to the proscenium performance, the same number as the immersive performance, were seated in a semi-circle on the stage. The actors were all on stage when the spectators walked in, and each performer was present in a different area (as indicated in Figure 2.4), silently embodying an action that was relevant to their character. The spectators seated themselves while listening to the sound of a ticking clock and watching the Young Woman seated centre stage, caressing a shawl.

The proscenium performance then unfolded as follows:

- *Scene One*: The journey of the Young Woman to the new country, focused on a conversation that takes place between her and the Immigration Official. This Official decides to place the Young Woman in a detention centre after being dissatisfied with her answers to his initial questions.

  Transition One: The sound of a ticking clock. The Young Woman silently changes out of her clothes into a prison uniform.

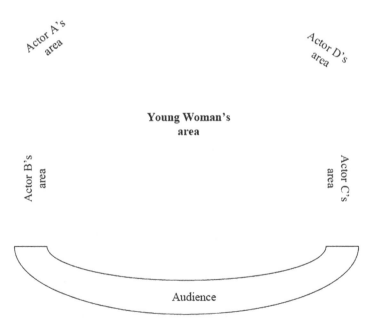

Figure 2.4 Map of the proscenium space

- *Scene Two*: The Young Woman is introduced to the Detention Centre Guard and her cellmate, the Fellow Detainee. She realizes that she cannot complain about anything while she is imprisoned.

  Transition Two: The sound of a ticking clock. The Young Woman writes letter after letter while saying the words "I would like to complain about. . . ." She rips each message off the notepad and throws it on the floor before beginning the next letter. The Young Woman starts her letter writing at a slow pace but eventually builds up her speed until she is writing frenetically. The floor is eventually covered with letters.

- *Scene Three*: The actor has a conversation with her Lawyer, who is characterized as someone who is sincerely looking out for the best interests of the Young Woman.

  Transition Three: The sound of a ticking clock. The Young Woman starts tearing up the letters, starting rapidly and then slowing down until she comes to a stop. The floor is now covered with shredded pieces of paper.

- *Scene Four*: A conversation between the Young Woman and the Guard. We understand that the protagonist is on a hunger strike. The Lawyer appears again and tells the Young Woman that her protest will not reflect well in her asylum application.

  Transition Four: The sound of a ticking clock. The Young Woman stuffs herself with dry cereal from a bowl. She eats until she cannot eat anything more; until she is almost retching.

- *Scene Five*: The Young Woman argues with the Guard for her right to take a shower.

  Transition Five: The sound of a ticking clock. The Young Woman enters the bathroom and we see her scream – the Guard is watching her in the shower. Her screams send the Guard away. The Young Woman takes off her uniform till all she is wearing are tights and an undershirt. She washes herself with water from a tub. She does so forcefully until she is almost clawing at her skin. She wants to wash off the gaze of the Guard. She eventually stops and puts her uniform back on.

- *Scene Six*: The Young Woman is informed by her Lawyer about the slow progress on her case.

  Transition Six: The sound of a ticking clock. The Young Woman prays.

- *Scene Seven*: A conversation that shows the camaraderie between the Young Woman and the Fellow Detainee.

  Transition Seven: The sound of a ticking clock. The Young Woman and the Fellow Detainee make paper chains together.

- *Scene Eight*: Another conversation between the Young Woman and the Immigration Official, in which her story is further questioned and dissected until she herself is unsure of what is true and what is not. The scene ends with her saying "I was ill. I was confused. I was . . . I was . . . I was. . . ."

  Transition Eight: The sound of a ticking clock. The Young Woman paces up and down while saying: "I was alone"; "I was scared"; "I was confused"; ending the transition with "I don't know why they didn't kill me. I wish they had."

- *Scene Nine*: The Fellow Detainee's application is denied and is deported. The Young Woman witnesses this.

  Transition Nine: The sound of a ticking clock. All her energy depleted, the Young Woman just sits on the floor and stares out in front of her.

- *Scene Ten*: The Lawyer and Immigration Official inform the Young Woman that she must leave the country.

  Transition Ten: The sound of a ticking clock. The Young Woman cleans up the stage, which is now littered with pieces of paper, water, and cereal. She packs up her things and changes out of her uniform, into the clothes with which she began the performance. She leaves behind the shawl that she was caressing at the beginning of the show and slowly walks out of the performance space.

This adaptation was staged in the College auditorium, a large space that has traditionally been associated with proscenium performances. The audience was seated on the stage so as to maintain a little more intimacy between the audience members and the performers, since the large size of the auditorium could have otherwise led to spatial distance itself being a potential variable in how audience members were affected by the piece. The auditorium also allowed for the performance to be complemented by the usage of lighting and sound: the Young Woman's area was lit by a spotlight and a rectangular corridor of light; each of the areas occupied by the other characters had its own kind of lighting: gobos of prison bars for the Guard and the Fellow Detainee; warm and harsh colours for the 'positive' and 'negative' characters of the Lawyer and the Immigration Official, respectively. Just as care was taken to design the space for the immersive performance, attention was given to the lighting and sound design for the proscenium adaption, to ensure that there was a comparable aesthetic 'standard' that was met in both the pieces.

In terms of rehearsals, the schedule for the proscenium performers involved meeting with the actors two (and occasionally, three) times a week. After initial table readings of the script, similarly to the immersive performers, proscenium actors were given character questionnaires to think through. These questionnaires were crafted before the script was edited a second time to have each actor play only one role, hence the allusion to multiple characters in Table 2.3.

Given the nature of this performance, after exploring characterization and ensuring actors' familiarization with the text, the rehearsals were focused on blocking and on integrating lighting and sound within the piece that was created. Once rehearsals ended, the first performance was for an audience of actors from the immersive performance before it was performed for the twelve spectators from the College who signed up to watch this show.

Table 2.3 Character questionnaires (proscenium adaptation)

Actors A, B, C, D	Young Woman
List each of the different characters that you play and alongside each, write down **one** unique trait that this character has. This unique trait could be an accent, a physical characteristic, a personality trait, or something else.	Describe how you met your husband – where did you go on your first date? What did you love most about him?
For each character that you play, list one costume element/object that you could use to differentiate that character from others – a scarf, a shawl, a jacket, a stick, a hat, sunglasses, and so on.	What was your relationship like with your mother, father, and sister? What is your favourite memory of your time together as a family? What did/do you love the most about where you are from?
For *each character* that you play, answer these questions: Why do your characters decide to pursue their chosen professions? *For example, why did the NURSE (Actor A) decide to take a job with the immigration centre?* How does your character feel about the young woman's situation? *For example, how does the CHILD-MAN (Actor C) feel about the young woman's situation?*	Who do you blame for the difficulties that you encounter with the immigration system in the new country – the guards, the doctors, or someone else? Why? If everything works out in terms of your asylum status, what are your aspirations for your life in your new country? When you are told that you have to return to your country, what are you most afraid of?

The performances

Spectators to both the performances were invited via email sign-ups, on a first-come, first-serve basis. This invitation informed the College community that there were only spots for twelve audience members at each performance and that each audience member would be requested to attend an hour-long group discussion the day after the performance, make entries in a journal for a month after the performance, and attend a thirty-minute individual interview a month after the performance. The invitation also included a content warning about the language and themes related to violence in the play. Though my initial email said nothing about the performances being different from each other, just that they would happen at different locations and at different times, it did seem that word had gotten out about 'participation' being the difference between the two shows. I learned through informal conversations and through certain replies to my email that some audience members had sought out actors' input and asked them which performance they should go to: some spectators wanted to make sure that they would get the chance to see their friends perform; others were just curious. And while most of the actors seemed to have maintained the confidentiality that they had agreed to, it did seem like there was some information that was also 'leaked'. In either case, both performances eventually had twelve spectators sign up for them, with a small number of spectators on a waitlist. While all twelve spectators (all students) showed up for the proscenium performance, only eleven of the twelve spectators (ten students + one faculty member) attended the immersive piece. I was told that the missing spectator had overslept on the morning of the performance.

Memo # 4

I knew from the get-go that trying to create two performances about the same theme, using different aesthetics, would be a difficult task. The creative process that was involved in a project like this was entirely new to me and there was one question that underscored my creative process: how would I ensure that both performances were 'created equal'?

Generally speaking, I believe that the two performances in this project were calibrated quite carefully and that the ways in which the immersive and proscenium pieces were designed make the feedback comparable, that is, everything else being

---

equal, any variance in audience/actor feedback from the two performances can (most likely) be attributed to the difference in the shows' aesthetics. That said, I must also acknowledge that particular choices I have made within the framework of each performance also have their own implications. For instance, the choice to place visual/image-based transitions between each of the scenes in the proscenium piece is likely to have created a different effect/affect than not having included these visuals at all. The choice to have one group of spectators wait in a waiting room while another went through their immersive experience could have resulted in differences for the spectator-participants who went first and those who went second. The choice to incorporate multiple actors, rather than sticking to the one-person structure as crafted by Adshead in her original script, could have had different implications for the proscenium piece. Performing the immersive piece in a building that the spectators were less familiar with (somewhere close to the College campus compared to a space on the campus, for instance) might have varyingly impacted the spectators' engagement with their environment. Placing the audience on the stage, closer to the actors, in the proscenium piece could have also led to different outcomes than placing them at a greater distance.

It is not so clear-cut, therefore, that everything was in fact 'created equal' in the two performances. And this possibility, in turn, means that some of the data generated from spectators and actors might not have anything to do with differences between proscenium and immersive aesthetics. Rather, variances in the data might have to do with specific choices that were made *within* those aesthetics. While I am aware of these challenges and their implications, I must also state that this particular conundrum – of everything being 'created equal' – is inevitably going to be an issue in any attempt to compare responses across theatrical forms. It is perhaps predictable then, that the data that is presented and analyzed in the following chapters is primarily used as a point of departure for generating new questions and for building new theories. The data does not provide certainties. Only allusions; directions; possibilities.

Onward then, to the data.

Works cited

Adshead, Kay. 2001. *The Bogus Woman.* London: Oberon Books.

Knowles, M. S. 1967. Program planning for adults as learners. *Adult Leadership.* 15:267–279.

Wang, E. E. 2011. Simulation and adult learning. *Disease-a-Month.* 57:664–678.

3 The data and the spectators

Memo #5

Before describing and analyzing the feedback that was gathered from the spectators, I would be remiss if I didn't mention what I expected their responses to be like. I expected to see a significant difference in how both groups of spectators would interpret their performances. While I hypothesized that they would interpret similar themes, I thought that the two groups of audience members would perceive the intention of the performances differently. I suspected that the 'affect' described would vary immensely between the two groups of spectators. I posited that, while the proscenium performance's audience members would identify to some extent with the character of the Young Woman protagonist, their affinity towards this character would not be as 'marked' or as 'intense' as the immersive piece's spectators' identification with the asylum seekers that they had to embody. I also postulated that spectators from the Immersive Theatre performance would make more journal entries than their proscenium theatre counterparts. These expectations were based on results that I saw in other simulation-based learning scenarios: concrete differences when there is a use of immersive strategies versus when there is not. The reality, then, was surprising because of the far more subtle points of comparison that emerged. The spectators' responses were surprising in all the avenues that were provided for gathering feedback: in their responses to the written questionnaires, in the ways in which they steered the focus group discussion, in the nature of their entries in their journal, and in how individual audience members interacted with me in the interviews.

Another expectation that manifested differently was the concern I had about a potential power dynamic emerging with the respondents. Even though my part-time status at the College during this experiment led to less power-based relationships with the participants than if I had been a full-time teacher who also saw many of these students in the classroom, the fact that the participants knew I would be teaching some of them in the future (I am a full-time employee at the College as of August 2016) could still have hampered their responses. However, while a power dynamic might have manifested for some of the spectators, I must note that I was (in general) pleased to see a degree of brutal honesty in how the students responded to the questions that I asked them. For example, there were some participants who said, "I just didn't think about the performance" and handed back empty journals to me. Others said a more diplomatic, "I didn't think about the performance that often and when I did, I didn't have the journal with me, so I haven't written much." The students did not seem to be preoccupied with being judged for their lack of entries in the journal, and though I must admit that it was hard to hear – that the performances had not been recalled as often as I hoped they would be – the actors and spectators seemed to be honest in how they did (not) remember the performances one month later.

In the initial stages of coding the data, I paid attention to the numbers. I calculated, within each question in the questionnaires, the numbers/proportion/percentage of responses that would show quantitative trends and patterns. However, while these numbers were initially useful in terms of familiarizing myself with the data, I realized that I was straying away the 'method of instances' that I discuss in Chapter 1 (about the conceptual framework). So, since the method of instances asks researchers to pay as much attention to one response as to another – as even one response can be analyzed to make larger comparisons and allusions in the spirit of theory-building rather than hypothesis confirmation – I began to distance myself from the numbers. As such, the reader will see that while I occasionally mention numbers in the data analysis, I also use terms like 'a majority', 'a large number', 'similar numbers', or 'one response' when making inferences from particular pieces of data. Wherever possible I also footnote the specific responses that were provided by the participants, so that the reader can look at the specific data from which I generate categories and proposals. I have attempted to give each piece of data its importance and try to create a coherent picture with the different puzzle pieces accounted for, even if one piece of the puzzle includes a response from only one person. Hence my considering the data analysis in the project to be as creative as it is analytical. As interpretive as it is logical.

This chapter is structured into sections that contain data that emerged from the four specific feedback mechanisms: the questionnaires, the group discussions, the individual interviews, and the journal entries. Each section includes an overview of the data that materialized, alongside brief discussions of my analyses of these emergences. A conversation that interweaves what seemed to emerge across the questionnaires, the focus group discussions, the individual interviews, and the journal entries – the data that I would like to highlight – is then further elaborated upon at the end of the chapter.[1] Before moving on to the data though I must reiterate that the process of data analysis has been a creative process of sorts, and my work as an Applied Theatre researcher-practitioner in places of war has influenced my interpretation and analysis of what emerged. Furthermore, it must be mentioned that I use some charged terminology in this chapter: terms like 'sympathy' and 'empathy', for example, which would require more unpacking in a traditional monograph. However, given that this book seeks to present a short-form approach to sharing this work, I have deliberately chosen *not* to unpack the terms. Not to mention that an extensive unpacking of these terms would require more finely targeted feedback mechanisms – not the general response formats that were created with the goals of this experiment in mind.

Data and the questionnaires

A day after the performance

The first question on the questionnaire that was given to both groups of audience members asked them to describe what they thought the *themes* of their performance were.[2] In analyzing the responses across both groups of spectators, there were three categories that emerged inductively: responses that spoke to themes about refugees/asylum seekers, responses that had to do with themes about immigration from a policy/government standpoint, and more abstract responses that mentioned emotions that had been evoked without necessarily linking these emotions to particular concepts or characters. In using this categorization to code the data, I found that most of the spectators to the immersive performance commented that their performance's themes had to do with refugees and asylum seekers. However, what was also notable was the large number of responses from this spectator group that also mentioned more abstract concepts without specifically mentioning the linkage between the concepts in question and issues surrounding refugees or asylum seekers.[3] Similarly, while most of the spectators to the proscenium performance also commented on themes related to refugee experiences and/or asylum seeking, a large number of these audience members also spoke to identifying themes related to the 'system'.[4] Additionally, a large number of responses in this group – akin to the Immersive Theatre spectators – also mentioned more abstract concepts and themes that did not directly relate to asylum-seeking or the system.[5]

An interesting difference in the spectators' responses to my question about theme, therefore, emerged in how 'policies' and 'systems' were/were not identified in the proscenium and immersive performances, respectively. Contrary to spectators from the proscenium performance,[6] the responses to the immersive piece included only two mentions of a policy/system-related thematic linkage. This difference between the two groups became interesting to me since it potentially suggests that while immersive spectators were focusing their attention on the emotive and character-based components of their performance, the proscenium spectators were able to both see the personal/emotional elements of the story shown to them, but were also able to identify structural (more 'bigger picture') issues that were being represented in the piece. Could this highlight a difference between the kinds of empathy that were generated in the two performances as a result of the different relationships between actor, character, and spectator in each aesthetic? This is a question that I will return to in this, and in following chapters.

The second question asked both groups of spectators about their interpretations' of the *intentions* of the creators in each performance – what did they think we wanted to evoke? Inductively, there were two categories that emerged in the data: responses that mentioned empathy, sympathy, or an emotion-focused intention were coded as feeling-based responses; responses that spoke to a less emotion-focused and more analytic intention (raising awareness was a popular one in this category) were coded as non-feeling-based responses. In response to this question then, apart from the multiple responses of the immersive performance being intended to evoke sympathy/empathy or raise awareness around the issues facing refugees and asylum speakers, many of the audience members spoke to 'negative'/uncomfortable experiences that they saw the performance as intending to generate: "fear" (Immersive Performance Spectator D, Questionnaire, 2016), "evoke outrage" (Immersive Performance Spectator I, Questionnaire, 2016), "uncomfortable" (Immersive Performance Spectator H, Questionnaire, 2016), and "loneliness [and] hunger" (Immersive Performance Spectator G, Questionnaire, 2016) were some of the ways in which the audience members described the intentions behind the immersive performance. The uncomfortable experiences described by the Immersive Theatre spectators relate to many existing critiques of the form: that the anxiety-inducing quality to Immersive Theatre makes the usage of the form questionable, especially in more volatile contexts. What is interesting is that this particular demographic – unlike, possibly, an already-anxious audience in a war zone – did not necessarily see discomfort as a negative outcome. In fact, some of the spectators who mentioned these discomfort-inducing responses were also those who asked (during the individual interviews) for the performance to be repeated. Regardless of how I interpret the spectators' attitude toward their discomfort though, it must be acknowledged that "an over aroused empathic response that creates personal distress (self-oriented and aversive)" could lead to "a turning-away from the provocative condition of the other" (Keen, 2006:208).

With regard to the same question of *intentions*, the proscenium piece's spectators highlighted something different.[7] While many responses from the proscenium performance's spectators similarly also described its intentions as being the generation of sympathy or empathy for refugees, or as seeking to raise awareness about the global refugee crisis, the interesting anomaly (from three of the twelve respondents) was that sympathy was not seen as being only intended for the character of the protagonist, i.e., the Young Woman. Rather, it was thought by these three spectators that the play also sought to inspire sympathy/empathy for the Lawyer, Detention Centre Guard, and the Immigration Official. These responses were framed as follows: "Make the audience pick the side of the young woman or that of the interrogators/guard/people who didn't believe her" (Proscenium Performance Spectator D, Questionnaire, 2016), "Sympathy for both sides of the argument" (Proscenium Performance Spectator H, Questionnaire, 2016), and "to show the perspective of the immigration official and how difficult it is for them to make decisions based on the stories they hear and to decide whether it is real" (Proscenium Performance Spectator J, Questionnaire, 2016).[8] Although these are only three responses that suggest a multi-dimensional sympathy, one-fourth of the total number of spectators, I believe that these reactions are interesting to consider when placed alongside responses to the first question about themes. I wonder, for instance, if the responses vis-à-vis the multi-perspective intentions of the proscenium performance – alongside the identification of state/policy-related themes more often than in the responses from the immersive piece's spectators – might evidence the evocation of a different kind of empathy by both performances.[9] Could the term 'critical empathy' be used to describe the responses from the spectators to the proscenium performance? Could we postulate that if the intentions of an Applied Theatre performance are to create an empathy/understanding for different sides, we would be better off using proscenium theatre? Is this different shade of empathy among the reasons why the binary between 'oppressor' and 'oppressed' that is drawn in the Theatre of the Oppressed (1985) becomes readily accepted by the spect-actor? This is to say: does participating within the performance create the conditions for an audience member to see one point of view more readily than any other? While a uniform identification with the 'victim' or the 'oppressed' might not seem problematic to some Applied Theatre practitioners, as someone who works often in the 'grey zones' (more on this in Dinesh, 2015b), this particular consideration around multi-dimensionality is important for me. If spectator-participants in immersive forms are more likely to be consumed by their own embodied experience (i.e., solely the shoes of the Other than they embody), might it indicate that – when the intention is to create an under-standing of various perspectives – another approach to immersion (closer to the proscenium model) might be what is desired?

As the third question on the questionnaires, audiences were asked to discuss the *most interesting element* from the performance that they were invited to.[10] Just more than half of the respondents to the Immersive Thea-tre performance mentioned finding a character in the performance to be the most interesting part of the show (particularly the character of the Fellow Detainee). Others mentioned their interest being drawn in by a strategy that had to with the chosen approach to Immersive Theatre: "being left alone" (Immersive Performance Spectator K, Questionnaire, 2016), "interaction between audience and performers" (Immersive Performance Spectator H, Questionnaire, 2016), "the building" (Immersive Performance Spec-tator E, Questionnaire, 2016), and the waiting room (Immersive Perfor-mance Spectator G, Questionnaire, 2016). While the audience members' interest in the immersive strategies was not surprising, what did surprise me was the number of responses that mentioned the Fellow Detainee as being the most interesting character compared even to the character that they themselves played. The reasons for the spectators' interest in the Fellow Detainee character included: "her acting and character [. . .] were the only parts of the performance that made me feel legitimately sad, she almost made me cry" (Immersive Performance Spectator A,

Questionnaire, 2016); "she was most illuminating as to what goes on with refugees [. . .] hearing what she had been through evoked empathy for refugees, when she was dragged out of the room, she left the picture of her child and food on the table. What was most powerful was then the lawyer came in, saw the mess and used the refugee's beloved photo to wipe the mess the orange left" (Immersive Performance Spectator B, Questionnaire, 2016); "I began to feel unhopeful for my process while hearing about her unjust case, how she was treated" (Immersive Performance Spectator C, Questionnaire, 2016); "because it was one character a lot of people could relate to the most. Especially when she showed the picture of her son" (Immersive Performance Spectator D, Questionnaire, 2016); "she was the perfect embodiment of hunger and desperation when she pulled out the apple from her purse and devoured it. At that moment, the performance became much more realistic" (Immersive Performance Spectator I, Questionnaire, 2016). Despite having had one-to-one interactions with different characters in their immersive experience, the Fellow Detainee was the only character that shared an experience similar to the persona given to the audience members. Was it that, given that audience members were surprised/discomfited/confused when being questioned by the Interrogator and the Lawyer, the character of the Fellow Detainee helped them fill in the gaps to their own story? Was it because the Fellow Detainee was the only character in the play who had as much/as little power as the audience member – all the other characters being much more powerful in terms of status within that immigration-based experience – thus inspiring a sense of comfort? Was it because the Fellow Detainee was the only character in the immersive experience that the audience member could most un-problematically empathize with? In trying to answer these questions I took on some research into narrative identification and empathy and I encountered existing conclusions that "one tends to be more empathic when there are similarities between the experiences of the empathizer and the target person and in the personalities of the two" (Corcoran, 1982:91). Given that the characters of the audience member-asylum seeker and the Fellow Detainee were 'cut from the same cloth', as it were, perhaps it is not surprising that spectators most identified with/found interesting the character that was like them but better informed about the experience. Furthermore, given the discomfort that was mentioned as being triggered, it is also possible that the spectators were exhibiting an expected response of, "in emotional events," paying "attention to other people on the scene" (Reisberg & Heuer, 1992:184). This tendency has been attributed to two reasons: "First, in an emotional situation, people in one's surround are themselves likely to become emotional, and it seems to us that others' emotion is an attention-grabbing stimulus of great force"; the second reason could be that "a considerable amount of 'social referencing' is likely to take place in emotional settings, as one seeks information in other faces – information about the event itself, and also about how one should react" (Reisberg & Heuer, 1992:184). The latter is perhaps most relevant in this case, given that the discomfort experienced by the spectator-asylum seeker when being questioned by the Interrogator and Lawyer is much more contextualized and socially referenced when placed in conversation with the experience of the Fellow Detainee.

While it was a character that seemed to most interest the spectators to the Immersive Theatre piece, in the proscenium performance more than half of the respondents mentioned finding the transitions/image-based elements to be the most interesting. While this might primarily be an insight into the aesthetic preferences of a particular student demographic, it is interesting to note that

> [n]arrative theorists, novel critics, and reading specialists have already singled out a small set of narrative techniques such as the use of first person narration and the interior representation of characters' consciousness and emotional states as devices supporting character identification, contributing to empathetic experiences, opening readers' minds to others, changing attitudes, and even predisposing readers to altruism.
>
> (Keen, 2006:213)

While these observations primarily refer to the experience of reading fiction, the propositions do seem to hold resonance with the proscenium spectators' responses in that when a "narrator self-narrates about his or her own experiences and perceptions" (like the Young Woman did in the transitions) there seemed to emerge "an especially close relationship between reader and narrative voice" (Keen, 2006:220). Since the transitions were the primary spaces in which the audience was allowed a visceral, less verbal, and interior representation of the protagonist, it was these spaces that seemed to elicit the most interest.

Next on the questionnaire, audiences were asked to discuss their opinions vis-à-vis the *authenticity* of the protagonist's story: their own character of the spectator-asylum seeker in the immersive piece and the character of the Young Woman in the proscenium piece.[11] While a majority of the spectators to the immersive performance were unsure as to the authenticity of the story of the character that they embodied, responses to the proscenium performance showed an equal split between those who believed the Young Woman's story, those who did not believe her story, and those who were unsure as to the veracity of the story. Upon looking at these responses in conversation with the answers to the first two questions about themes and intentions, I have come to wonder if it was the relative distance afforded by the proscenium piece that allowed the audience members to come to more firm decisions about the authenticity of the protagonist's story. While I shall return to this point later in this chapter, it is also worth mentioning the distinction that Bruce McConachie (2008:99) proposes between empathy and sympathy: where empathy means an imagination of "stepping into an actor/character's shoes," whereas "sympathy involves projecting her or his own beliefs and feelings onto the stage figure." If one were to take this argument further in light of the audience members' responses to authenticity, could the relative degree of certainty in the proscenium spectators' responses imply the ability to project their own beliefs onto the stage figure, creating the conditions for sympathy rather than empathy? Could this distinction also help explain why the immersive spectators were unable to find a more certain response since so much of their experience was about (literally) stepping into the character's shoes?

As the fifth question, audience members were asked to choose between four options as to how they had been *affected* by the performance; they were allowed to choose more than one response. The first option said, "I am better informed about the experiences of refugees and asylum seekers"; the second option was "I encountered an interesting story"; the third option was "I want to help refugees and asylum seekers," and the final "Other" option allowed audience members to list something that was not provided as an option. In response, 70 per cent of the respondents to the Immersive Theatre option chose: "I am better informed about the experiences of refugees and asylum seekers" i.e., they chose this answer either in isolation or in combination with one or more of the other options that were presented to them. On the contrary, 75 per cent of the respondents to the proscenium performance said that the second option – "I encountered an interesting story" – best captured how they had been affected. The embodied action of being involved in the story seemed to lead to the immersive piece's audience members to think that they had gained new information about refugee/asylum seeking experiences while the proscenium piece generated a response that was quite different in that audience members explicitly mentioned having *not* encountered new information (this will be further evidenced when discussing what emerged during the focus group discussions). The contrast between the two groups of responses suggests that there might be potential in considering if/how the embodiment of an Other leads to a spectator's perception of information gain. That said, it must be acknowledged that this notion of information gain can be hugely problematic, with spectators assuming that their one hour of being in an Other's shoes gives them 'knowledge' about that experience – much like the kind of tourist who speaks patronizingly about 'knowing' a local culture after spending a few days at its touristic sites. However, without losing sight of these ethical questions, the 'information gain' versus the 'story-telling' differences in audience member's reactions to the two performances does seem to warrant more consideration.

Next, audiences were asked to rank four statements in order of importance, each of which mentioned one *outcome* as being most important in addressing the current, real-world global refugee crisis: *Empathy, Activism, Information*, and *Policy Reform*.[12] Sixty per cent of the spectators to the immersive performance said that *Information* about the global refugee crisis was the least relevant in addressing the issues at hand – an interesting contrast with the answer to the previous question in which a majority had said that gaining more information about the refugee experience was what had most occurred for them through the immersive experience. Could it be that living in the shoes of the asylum seeker made the spectator-participants feel the futility of knowing more, without the ability to 'do' something with that information? There does seem to be some justification for this argument since the largest number of consistent responses from the spectators to the immersive performance said that *Policy Reform* is what is most important in addressing the current refugee crisis – perhaps an outcome of having to wait for long periods of time and experience, kinaesthetically, the inefficiencies of bureaucracy?

For the spectators to the proscenium performance, both *Empathy* and *Policy Reform* were seen equally as being the most relevant strategies to address the global refugee crisis, while *Activism* and *Information* were tied in being seen as least relevant in addressing the global refugee crisis. What is interesting to note is that *Policy Reform* was seen as being most relevant by *both* groups of spectators just as *Information* was seen as being least relevant by both groups. Therefore, despite both groups of spectators exhibiting different shades of sympathy/empathy/critical empathy in response to previous questions, this did not seem to cause much of a difference in terms of the real-world steps that they assessed as being necessary to address the issues that were performed. Of course, it is also entirely possible that the similarity in these responses has nothing to do with the performances themselves but rather indicates something about the student body at this college. The student body is (generally) idealistic and is encouraged, by the ideologies of the institution and by the staff, to think about big-picture changes to solve problems. Perhaps this prevalent desire 'to change the world', alongside pre-existing knowledge about the global refugee crisis, is what ultimately shaped the spectator's responses to this particular question.

Finally, the last question on the questionnaire asked spectators to comment on the notion of *identification*, i.e., which character in the particular performance that they watched/participated in provoked a personal memory for them.[13] Since this question was optional and spectators could choose to not respond if they did not identify with any character in the piece, what was also of interest to me was how many audience members from each performance even attempted to answer this question. Seventy per cent of the spectators to the immersive performance responded to this question and mentioned identifying with/relating to different characters in the piece – contrary to my expectation that they would mostly identify with the character that they themselves were embodying.[14] Apart from one audience member who most identified with the character that they played, others mentioned different characters within the immersive experience as having evoked personal memories for them. Furthermore, while a majority of the immersive spectators answered this question, only one-third of the audience members to the proscenium performance provided answers, and all these respondents mentioned associations with particular aspects of the Young Woman's character. These outcomes might be seen as being in conversation with the response to the second question on intentions, where it was the proscenium performance's spectators that indicated a potential empathy/sympathy for characters other than the protagonist. Could it be then, that while proscenium spectators were able to see multi-dimensionality in intention more visibly than their Immersive Theatre counterparts, the personal associations drawn from different characters within the performances remained more significant for the Immersive Theatre spectators? Of course, I must acknowledge here that framing the concept of identification as being based on the generation of a personal memory is itself a very specific choice, and had I framed the concept another way, different results might have been observed. That said, given the existing framing of identification and the results that emerged, I looked into the realm of autobiographical memory to gain some insight into why/how involuntary memories emerge in response to a stimulus. In so doing, research suggests that "[i]nvoluntary memories assist knowledge transfer from a past to a present situation (i.e., from the remembered event to the situation in which the memory arises)" (Berntsen, 2012:302). While "this relevance may [sometimes] be as simple as helping the person to recognize and contextualize the memory cue," it is not always the case; rather, in "other times, it may assist the person in better orienting in his or her physical and social environment, and becoming aware of changes and potential dangers [. . .] and it may support analogical reasoning" (Berntsen, 2012:302). Furthermore, in "a social context, an involuntary memory may move the person to tell other people about the remembered event and thereby facilitate entertainment and social bonding." Also, "an involuntary memory may instigate a direct change in an ongoing activity or suggest a solution to a problem and thus hold a directive function" (Bernsten & Rubin, 2012:302–303).

While I cannot make claims about what function the involuntary memories necessarily indicate within the context of this project, this difference between the two groups' responses does seem to warrant further consideration – a future avenue of investigation that might require a more careful articulation of different dimensions to identification.

Data and the group discussions

A day after the performance

There were four different next-day discussion sessions: one with the actors in the immersive performance, one with the actors in the proscenium piece, and one for each of the spectator groups. These sessions began with the participants being asked to sign consent forms and to fill out questionnaires, after which there was a discussion that followed. In this discussion, after an introduction as to how the session would function, participants were asked to pose questions to each other rather than my posing questions to them, i.e., the discussion would be facilitated by the respondents themselves. Through this strategy, I was hoping to ascertain what was most present on the different participants' minds without my own agendas guiding their conversation. While I occasionally intervened in the discussions when there seemed to be a lull in the conversation or when I needed to clarify statements that were unclear, for the most part I remained an observer and looked for trends within the questions and discussion topics that were brought up. The discussion sessions concluded with the distribution of journals and with the invitation for each participant to sign up for individual interviews in a month, at which point they would be asked to return their journals.

The first question that was posed in the immersive performance's spectator group, by one of the audience members, was to ask the group how different individuals felt upon leaving the performance space. In response to this question spectators shared their personal experiences of the performance: some mentioned personal emotions that had been evoked, others talked about the way in which props had been used in significant ways (the photo that one Fellow Detainee had brought in and left behind when being taken out of the room, for example), others spoke about the hunger that the video in the waiting room had created for them, and a few spectators discussed their reactions to the characterization of the Interrogators, Waiting Room Guards, Lawyers, and Fellow Detainees. This occurrence parallels what has been documented about Punchdrunk, a UK-based theatre company, that "communicating immersive experience has an interesting connection with Punchdrunk's emphasis on individual journey" and that "splitting up means a spectator can learn about not only their own experience but that of their companions" (Biggin, 2015:309). In this vein, the spectators to the immersive adaptation of *The Bogus Woman* – much like Punchdrunk's audience members – wanted to know what their peers had/had not experienced. These thoughts about subjective experiences of the performance led into a discussion about specific audience members' personal experiences with visa issues and furthermore, two members of the audience brought up the similarity between the immersive performance and particular kinds of video games that they played. The discussion veered to elements in the design (the posters) that were used in the different passageways of the building, and the audience members swapped notes about what they had noticed and what they had not understood. Soon, the spectators began to pose questions to me. They asked me about the differences between directing an immersive show and a more conventional performance and also asked me why I had not acted in the show myself. They wanted to know more about the info-mercial that was screened in the waiting room and inquired about whether or not we had back-up plans in place for unexpected responses. The specta-tors from the immersive performance also posed questions about whether I would have invited audience members with real experiences of being refugees/asylum seekers and expressed an interest in knowing more about the proscenium performance that they had not watched. The participants' questions highlighted the importance of novelty in their experience of spec-tatorship within the immersive piece and how that novelty engendered a curiosity not only about the experiences of other spectators but about also the experience of those who created the piece.

The discussion among the spectators who came to the proscenium perfor-mance began very differently with one of the participants asking everyone else: "Who thought the story was actually true?" (Proscenium Performance Spectator A, Group Discussion, 2016). A long discussion followed about the veracity of the Young Woman's story and about whether or not it mattered if her story was true or false. This discussion about authenticity evolved into a debate about the need for stricter immigration policies in the current global climate, with students arguing both for and against the need for more severe security checks. Then, one student asked "Did you think [the story occurred] on any particular continent?" (Proscenium Performance Specta-tor B, Group Discussion, 2016) – a question that stimulated a discussion about the possible real-world contexts to which the play could be applica-ble; a discussion that eventually returned to the question of the authenticity of the Young Woman's story. Since the conversation reached a lull when similar arguments about truth and falsehood re-emerged, I posed a question and asked the spectators about the place for a theatre/art in the face of a very real and current global refugee crisis. At this point the discussion shifted to a consideration of appropriate target audiences for such works and the participants debated about whether or not the community at the College was indeed a suitable spectator group for the proscenium performance. Some of the audience members seemed to be of the opinion that much of the College community was already informed about the refugee crisis and as such, the proscenium performance did not show them anything that they did not already know. Thus, these participants believed that the proscenium performance might have been better targeted toward a different audience, one that might be less aware about these affairs than themselves. This particular observation differed from the reactions of the immersive performance's spectators who did not exhibit any doubts about whether or not they should have been an audience to their piece, although these spectators were probably just as well/ill-informed about the refugee crisis as their peers. Was it the immersive form, in particular, that enabled this difference to occur? Or was it the presence of novelty that encouraged the immersive performance's spectators to display more curiosity in response to pre-existing knowledge?

A difference in curiosity levels is not only apparent in the two groups' understanding of information gain, but it is also observable in the immersive performance's participants wanting to know more about each other's experiences while the proscenium piece's spectators focused on questions of truth versus falsehood. In order to refine my understanding of these occurrences I examined the existing scholarship on diverse types of interest and found two points of resonance: situational interest and topic interest. Could the curiosity shown by the immersive performance's spectators be termed situational interest – where such an interest is seen as being "elicited by aspects of a situation, such as novelty or intensity, and by the presence of a variety of human interest factors contributing to the attractiveness of different types of content"? (Tobias, 1994:38). Since "novelty and surprise produced by [a] precipitating event is a necessary condition for situational interest to emerge" (Rotgans & Schmidt, 2014:38), did the immersive form evoke situational interest simply because it was novel to this particular spectator group? Or is situational interest the type of curiosity that is generated by all immersive forms? Or does situational interest simply depend on novelty, i.e., any form that is more unfamiliar/novel within a particular setting is likely to evoke situational interest? Similar questions are raised when the concept of 'topic interest' is applied to the engagement displayed by the proscenium performance's spectators. Since topic interest "refers to peoples' relatively enduring preferences for different topics, tasks, or contexts" (Tobias, 1994:38), could it be that the particular topic of authenticity evidenced the preferences of some, more talkative individuals in the proscenium piece's spectator group? Or, are all proscenium performances likely to generate more topic interest rather than situational interest? While the concepts of situational and topic interest seem relevant toward understanding what occurred in the discussions the day after the performance, an exploration of diverse kinds of interest vis-à-vis specific aesthetics emerges as an area that needs more investigation.

Data and the individual interviews

A month after the performance

One month after the performances all participants were invited to sign up for individual interviews. While a majority of the spectators from both performances attended their interviews, there were a few individuals who chose not to attend (more information on the numbers later in this discussion). The individual interviews began with my asking the spectators what they remembered about the performance itself, followed by asking if they had any comments about the process of making entries in the journal and if they saw any patterns in what made them recall the performance in the intervening month. Finally, spectators were asked if they had anything to add and/or if they wanted to pose any questions to me.

The responses from the spectators to the immersive performance involved a whole range of memories: from characters, to the setting, to the waiting, to post-performance reflections that had occurred about personal experiences with immigration, or thoughts about what the spectator-participants wished they could have done differently in their role as asylum seekers. Similarly, during the individual interviews with the spectators to the proscenium performance, respondents spoke to remembering the general trajectory and themes of the piece, the sound of the ticking clock, the transitions and scenes that included visual imagery, the staging, and the feeling that came from being so close to the actors. It was evident that, in terms of memory, there did not seem to be a significant difference between how the two performances remained/not in spectators' recollections. When asked at the end of the interview if they had any additional comments, proscenium spectators brought up questions about the purpose of this experiment, about the way in which the use of 'time' in the performance had been affective/effective, and interestingly, about whether a prior interest in issues of asylum-seeking and refugees might have played a role in how the performance was retained and remembered by spectators. In a similar fashion the spectators to the immersive performance asked questions about the aesthetics in their experience, requested me to do more performances like this in the future (both within and outside the College), and enquired when the results of this experiment would be shared with them.

A particularly interesting insight during the individual interviews came from one spectator to the immersive performance, who attributed her responses within the piece as being linked to personal relationships that she had/did not have with the actors playing the Lawyer and the Interrogator in her interrogation room. With regard to the relationship between actor/character and spectator, it is useful to draw from McConachie who argues (in Helms, 2012:94) that spectators "do not need to suspend their disbelief because they are aware of actors and characters not as wholly discrete entities but as part of a single conceptual blend, the actor/character." As such, "though the spectator is aware of this blend and can consciously manipulate it (choosing to alternate focus between the actor and the character), the cognitive processes that connect spectators to actor/characters are largely automatic and unconscious" (Helms, 2012:94). Clearly this notion of the actor/character blend becomes further complicated in a process like Immersive Theatre, where the spectators are not only responding to the actor/characters around them, but they are also dealing with their own blend of being actor, character, and spectator. Furthermore, in experiments like this one, where both spectators and actors come from within the same 'closed' community, the actor/character blend is even more complicated by a relationship/knowledge of the other that predates the performance itself. So, no longer is it simply the character/actor blend that affects spectators in such performances, but it is also the blend between the identities of the individual as person, the individual as actor, the individual as character, and the individual as spectator. As I mentioned, this point first emerged as being relevant when the aforementioned spectator did not personally know the actor playing the Interrogator in her immersive scenario. Despite the College being a fairly small community, the spectator moved in different circles than this performer and, as a result, was more unnerved by the aggression of the Interrogator. Furthermore, this same spectator also mentioned a previously uncomfortable encounter between her and the actor playing the Lawyer in her scenario; a relationship history that she attributed to heightening the discomfort that she experienced during the performance. In reflecting on this spectator's ruminations I came to wonder if a pre-existing familiarity between the actor and the participant in an immersive context might be implicated in how the experiment stays with its spectators. I had initially made this choice, of having actors and audience members from the same College community, for two reasons: primarily for the convenience that came from having captive audience of performers and spectators; secondarily, as a way to possibly address the ethical questions of making spectators vulnerable to strangers. However, this spectator's question led me to reconsider the impacts of spectators (not) knowing their actors in an Immersive Theatre experience.

The question of personal relationships is not relegated solely to immersive performances, of course, and spectators and actors in the proscenium performance also highlighted this concern about pre-existing relationships. That said this concern was framed very differently from the proscenium performance's respondents for whom the question seemed to emerge primarily during the Young Woman's transition scenes where she engages in actions that highlight the fragility of her condition. For example, in one transition, the Young Woman strips down from her everyday clothes into a prison uniform in view of the audience. And during this transition, both the actor playing the Young Woman and a couple of spectators who knew the performer personally seemed to encounter discomfort. While exploring the reasons for this discomfort and analyzing the impact of pre-existing relationships in proscenium pieces might yield exciting insights, I am primarily interested in the manifestation of the person/ actor/ character/ spectator blend in Immersive Theatre: how might spectator-participants to immersive experiences be affected differently based on whether or not they know the performers? In one sense it seems logical to assume that spectator-participants feel safer when they know their actors, given how vulnerable an immersive experience makes its audience members. Conversely though, it is equally likely that actors and spectators who know each other will bring in the histories of their personal relationships into the theatrical scenario; as Martin Barker (in Reason & Reynolds, 2010:50) says, "audiences bring their social and personal histories with them."

When thinking about this spectator's response and the questions it provokes in conjunction with my ongoing work in a conflict zone like Kashmir, I am now considering how one negotiates this knowing/not-knowing of actors and spectator-participants in an Immersive Theatre experience. Rather than seeking a one-size fits all response though, I have come to wonder what kinds of immersive experiences would benefit from different degrees of familiarity, or lack thereof, between spectators and performers. For instance, in one condition of Stanley Milgram's obedience experiments (1961; in Perry, 2013), the teacher-volunteer administering the shocks and the learner-actor receiving the shocks (who had been previously informed that the shocks would not be real) were individuals who had a pre-existing relationship. Unlike the relatively high numbers of teacher-volunteers that administered shocks to learner-actors who were strangers to them, the condition in which they knew each other revealed that "when people genuinely believed someone was being hurt – and it was someone close to them – they refused to continue" (Perry, 2013:178).[15] Similarly, Philip Zimbardo (2007:25) has also noted in the Stanford Prison Experiment that "conditions that make us feel anonymous, when we think that others do not know us or care to, can foster antisocial, self-interested behaviors" (Zimbardo, 2007:25). Since the immersive qualities to these two social psychology experiments share resonances with Immersive Theatre scenarios (as explained in the introduction), Milgram and Zimbardo's observations only serve to underscore the questions about identity that were raised in this project, questions that I would like to explore in future experiments.

Data and the journal entries

A month after the performance

The second question that I asked during the individual interviews was about how the spectators found the process of keeping the journal and what kinds of stimuli had provoked them to make entries. With the Immersive Theatre experience there were varied responses: one spectator spoke about a greater urge to write during the first two weeks after the performance; others mentioned that it was easy to find stimuli that brought up the performance because of seeing actors around the College campus, or because of immigration-related topics that were brought up in their classes, or because of video games that they played. Others, very honestly, said that they had not thought of the performance at all; some others spoke about not always having had access to the journal when a memory of the performance emerged; one audience member (the only faculty member spectator whose office had been used as one of the interrogation offices in the piece) spoke to thinking about the performance every time she entered her office.

In terms of the diary entries from the immersive performance's spectators, there was a total of thirty entries that were made by the ten participants who came to the interviews: one spectator did not sign up for an interview; one had missed the performance itself. There were nine entries that were made in the week immediately following the performance and five entries were made during the second week after the performance. This second week also happened to coincide with Project Week, a weeklong experiential education program that took College students to different parts of the United States on short trips that were focussed on diverse topics/projects: hiking, juvenile justice, working with a relief group on the US-Mexico border, a migration themed film festival in Mexico, mining in the south-western United States, and so on.

Almost half of the total number of journal entries therefore took place in the first two weeks following the performance. Of the remaining half there were five that were not dated, making it difficult to ascertain any patterns. Apart from the dates on which the entries were made, in analyzing the content, I attempted to discern the specific kinds of stimuli that audience members attributed to their having made entries in the journal: what had made them think about the performance? While there were a small number of entries in which the stimulus was unclear, a majority of the notes clearly indicated the stimulus that had triggered the memory of the immersive

Table 3.1 Overview of immersive spectators' journal entries

Spectator	Stimulus [DIRECT/INDIRECT]
A	1. Reflecting on the performance while on an outdoor/hiking expedition on Project Week **[INDIRECT]**
B	1. Emotions on the day following the performance **[INDIRECT]** 2. A dream about the performance **[INDIRECT]** 3. A self-reflection inspired by an impending Project Week departure **[INDIRECT]** 4. Camping during Project Week: this student's Project Week had to do with mining issues in New Mexico; nothing overtly related to issues around immigration or asylum seeking **[INDIRECT]** 5. Bus breaking down during Project Week **[INDIRECT]** 6. Travelling during Project Week **[INDIRECT]** 7. The landscape on Project Week **[INDIRECT]** 8. Taking a shower and having a good meal upon returning from Project Week **[INDIRECT]** 9. Mid-term exams **[INDIRECT]** *Entries 10, 11, 12, and 13 mentioned the same stimulus – the impending interview with me – as having functioned as a reminder of the performance; counted as four separate entries since they were made on different dates.* **[DIRECT]**
C	1. Crossing the border between the US and Mexico on Project Week **[DIRECT]** 2. A class in which the refugee crisis was being discussed **[DIRECT]** 3. The spectator's office as being a constant stimulus **[DIRECT]** 4. Interactions with other spectators as being stimulus **[DIRECT]** *All responses above were listed as one undated entry and were written as quick reflections the day prior to the spectator's individual interview (as mentioned by the spectator); hence counted as one DIRECT entry.*
D	1. Skype conversation with a friend **[INDIRECT]** 2. A friend being scammed on Project Week **[INDIRECT]** 3. Family friend adopting a baby **[INDIRECT]** 4. Easter holidays **[INDIRECT]** 5. A school sponsored retreat about engaging with conflict **[INDIRECT]**
E	1. Seeing an actor form the show **[DIRECT]** 2. A class in which the topic of immigration was discussed **[DIRECT]**
F	1. Stories about refugees on Facebook **[DIRECT]** 2. Being rejected from Colleges that this second year student had applied to **[INDIRECT]** 3. Thinking of home **[INDIRECT]**

(*Continued*)

Table 3.1 (Continued)

Spectator	Stimulus [DIRECT/INDIRECT]
G	1. Emotions the day after the performance **[INDIRECT]**
	2. A scene from a TV series having to do with immigration **[DIRECT]**
	3. A dream **[INDIRECT]**
	4. Seeing the journal itself **[DIRECT]**
H	1. Unclear what the stimulus was **[UNCLEAR]**
	Two audience members did not make any entries in their journals.

performance for each particular audience member.[16] While Table 3.1 provides an overview of the responses, there were some particularly interesting occurrences that warrant mention. Two of the respondents spoke about having dreamt of the performance and mentioned the dream as having become the stimulus that evoked an entry into the journal. Ten out of the thirty responses mentioned a 'direct' stimulus that reminded them of the experience – by direct I mean entries that were inspired by running into an actor from the play, by news stories talking about the refugee crisis, by Facebook posts that had to do with refugee-related narratives, or by Project Week experiences that took students to the US-Mexico border and had them engage very obviously with the theme of immigration. A greater number of the entries, however, seemed to be inspired by what I'm terming '*in*direct' stimuli (nineteen out of thirty), i.e., responses that mentioned the participants' recalling the performance because of a self-reflective application of the experience, without a direct link to themes around refugees, immigration, or asylum seeking.

When dealing with the proscenium performance's spectators, responses to my questions about the journal process revealed answers including the role that Project Week–related stimuli had played in recalling the performance: the obligation and guilt that were felt by a couple of respondents for not writing in the journal; honest admissions about the performance not having come up for some spectators; challenges identifying the stimulus that had caused the performance to be recalled; classes in which the refugee crisis had been discussed and that had led to respondents thinking about the performance; seeing actors on campus and that being a stimulus in recalling the performance; and finally, one respondent spoke to the question of representation in the journal, i.e., since the spectators knew that I was going to be reading their journal entries, that there were always considerations

Table 3.2 Overview of proscenium spectators' journal entries

Spectator	Stimulus [DIRECT/INDIRECT]
A	1. Emotions the day after the performance **[INDIRECT]** 2. Conversation with friends about Danish immigration policy **[DIRECT]** 3. **UNCLEAR** stimulus
B	1. Cereal in the dining hall (that had been used as a prop in one of the transitions) **[DIRECT]** 2. Seeing one of the actors from the performance around campus **[DIRECT]** 3. Class in which immigration was discussed **[DIRECT]**
C	1. Self-reflection about the performance **[INDIRECT]** 2. Lyrics to a song **[INDIRECT]** 3. Being in New Orleans on Project Week **[INDIRECT]** 4. Working with a non-governmental organization on Project Week **[INDIRECT]** 5. An activity during Project Week **[INDIRECT]** 6. Mother's birthday **[INDIRECT]** 7. Spanish class assignment **[INDIRECT]**
D	1. Self-reflection about the performance **[INDIRECT]** 2. Class in which immigration was discussed as a topic **[DIRECT]**
E	1. US presidential election debates about immigration **[DIRECT]** 2. Conversation about torture with peers **[DIRECT]** 3. Dealing with immigration at an airport during Project Week **[DIRECT]**
F	1. Conversation about family **[INDIRECT]** 2. Being at the US-Mexico border on Project Week **[DIRECT]** 3. A co-curricular activity, Amnesty, in which the group had chosen to focus on Syrian refugee policy **[DIRECT]**
G	1. Discussion about the performance **[DIRECT]** 2. Self-reflection **[INDIRECT]** 3. Discussion in economics class about refugees **[DIRECT]** 4. **UNCLEAR** stimulus 5. Book about migration **[DIRECT]**
H	1. Conversation about immigration **[DIRECT]** 2. Operation Streamline and learning about it at the US-Mexico border **[DIRECT]**
I	1. Watching a film about immigration **[DIRECT]**

One audience member did not make any entries in their journal.

around what to write and what not to include. There were a total of twenty-nine entries from ten participants (two audience members did not sign up for the individual interviews) and most of the entries took place in the first two weeks after the performance (eighteen out of the twenty-nine entries). There were about five entries in the third week after the performance, after which the number of entries dropped off (two per week). In looking at the kinds of stimuli that were recorded in the journal entries, apart from one participant (who also was the one who made the most – seven – individual entries) that stated different indirect stimuli as causing her to remember/recall the performance, most others' entries mentioned more direct stimuli as having provoked a remembrance of the play: sixteen out of twenty-nine entries were classified as containing such direct stimuli; eleven out of twenty-nine were entries alluded to indirect stimuli *but* seven of these eleven entries were from the same audience member, and two entries had unclear stimuli See Table 3.2.

In attempting to understand how these aforementioned trends of direct and indirect stimuli might be analyzed, I commenced an investigation into the cognitive functions that underlie particular kinds of learning. And upon considering the many different proposals that are suggested in existing scholarship, there was one articulation that became particularly helpful. This proposal delineates between "two types of memory organization, conceptual and associative" where conceptual organization involves the grouping of items of information "according to a principled taxonomic system [. . .] For example: cow, horse, dog; milk, wine, water; bucket, glass, barrel" (Koriat & Melkman, 1987:173). This is to say that items are grouped according to a larger concept: animals, liquids, and containers in the example mentioned. In comparison, however, associative organization is said to use a way of organizing information in which "members of a group are associatively related without constituting members of the same conceptual class" (Koriat & Melkman, 1987:173). So, in this mode of organization the associations might look like "cow, milk, bucket; grapes, wine, barrel; horse, coach, whip" where the grouping is based on before the word "direct [. . .] associations among the members in a group" (Koriat & Melkman, 1987:173). In these forms of associative organization, the "associations may be of many different sorts, with no systematic principle of relatedness that cuts across the system of grouping as a whole" (Koriat & Melkman, 1987:173). Using this delineation then, we might understand that "associative groupings rest on direct links, whereas conceptual groupings rest on indirect, mediated links" (Koriat & Melkman, 1987:173). This framework clearly has parallels with the analyses of the journal entries: while spectators to the proscenium performance seemed to be more likely to use a form of associative processing (seeing an actor from the performance → thinking about the performance

→ writing in the journal), spectators to the immersive performance seemed to be more likely to use a form of conceptual processing (experiencing loneliness on Project Week → reflecting on loneliness during the performance → writing in the journal). Furthermore, in comparing the two forms of processing, it has been suggested that "deep processing appears to encourage conceptual organization [that leads] to better long-term retention than associative organization" while "associative organization appears to yield more superior memory performance than conceptual organization" (Koriat & Melkman, 1987:180). Would these proposals around conceptual versus associative processing imply that a proscenium performance might be a more effective/affective strategy when the intention is to create associative recalls for spectators? Similarly, would immersive performances be the strategy to use when the theatre maker's intention is for a piece to stimulate conceptual connections? These are questions that need some further investigation.

Highlights from the data

Each of the particular feedback processes implemented with the spectators suggests particular concepts that might help delineate immersive and proscenium experiences. And although this data cannot be generalized toward all such aesthetic efforts, what the data might allow for is an identification of the theories that a theatre practitioner-researcher might benefit from considering when choosing such forms. Again, I must mention that I choose to highlight those ideas that have particular relevance to my work as an Applied Theatre researcher-practitioner in places of war – a relevance that I will discuss briefly in the *Memos* that end this chapter, and more extensively in the conclusions.

First, the questionnaires indicate that the two performances generated *different shades of empathy*: that proscenium performances might more likely lead to a distanced empathy, akin to sympathy, that allows a multi-dimensional interpretation; that immersive performances seem to cause emotion-based empathy that is more likely to evoke autobiographical memories for spectators. The questionnaires also reveal that, in an immersive experience, audience members are likely to be drawn toward *another sympathetic character* – one that references the spectators' own character and provides insights into how they might navigate their experience. Second, the focus group discussions indicate that there are (potentially) different kinds of interest that are generated through the two different aesthetic approaches in this project. The immersive piece seemed to generate situational interest where the spectators' interest was oriented toward the ways in which individual audience members, and their peers, negotiated their respective immersive situations. In contrast the proscenium piece seemed to generate topic interest, where spectators constantly returned to the topic of authenticity and whether or not the story of the protagonist could be trusted. The *different kinds of interest* that might be generated by specific aesthetic forms are, therefore, another avenue for a theatre practitioner-researcher to consider. Third, the individual interviews brought up the notion of *identity* – of the implications of having personal relationships define how actors/spectators ultimately respond to each other regardless of the aesthetic. Finally, the journals suggest that a *different type of processing* seemed to occur for the spectators to the two different performances: a more conceptual processing for the immersive spectators for whom indirect stimuli more often led to recalling the performance; a more associative processing for the proscenium spectators for whom direct stimuli more often seemed to cause a recall of the performance. This is not to say that one type of processing is more generally desirable than the other, but simply that these forms of processing might have longer-term repercussions on spectators' post-performance responses.

Memo #6

In thinking about how to take these highlighted insights further, I return to my personal repertoire as a theatre maker who works with Immersive Theatre in places of war:

Different shades of empathy

- What are the cultural and contextual factors that impact empathy?
- What shade of empathy might be most useful in an Applied (Immersive) Theatre intervention that seeks to stimulate debate/ activism/ learning/ behavioural change, as the case may be?
- Which approach to framing empathy would better allow for controversial narratives to be showcased without antagonizing spectators who hold a different political position from those that are being performed?

Presence of a sympathetic character

- Can the intentional inclusion of a sympathetic character help address the anxiety that might arise for spectators from the use of immersive aesthetics?
- How much similarity needs to be maintained between the character being embodied by the spectator-participant and the accompanying sympathetic character that they draw some comfort from?
- Does the inclusion of such a sympathetic character alter the implications of pre-existing relationships between actors and audience members, in a conflict zone in particular?

Types of interest

- How do we better understand the role of novelty in generating interest in an Applied Theatre intervention?
- Do spectators respond differently, in terms of the interest that they demonstrate, based on whether the novelty lays within the form or within the content?
- Are certain kinds of interest more likely to be generated by specific aesthetic forms, regardless of the presence/absence of novelty?

Actors/spectators (not) knowing each other

- In a war zone, where the work often involves raising contentious themes, are there particular kinds of aesthetics that would benefit from an existing relationship between performer and audience member?
- What are the kinds of performances in which it might be integral for the actor and the spectator to be strangers?
- Do questions about a pre-existing relationship between performers and audience members hold more poignancy for immersive aesthetics, or are they equally relevant for all theatrical genres?

Conceptual versus associative processing

- Could such delineation assist Applied Theatre practitioners to reach a better understanding of the longer-term repercussions from theatrical work in places of war?

- Could a better understanding of cognitive processes help address the concern of many Applied Theatre projects, of re-traumatizing already-anxious spectators?
- How are cognitive processes impacted by particular cultural backgrounds?

As I mentioned in the Memo that began this chapter, I expected to see more 'obvious' differences in how the two groups of spectators responded to their performances. A difference in the number of journal entries, for example. Or a difference in what each group would assess as being a necessary real-world strategy to address the global refugee crisis. Or a difference in how much was remembered about each performance. Instead, what I encountered was subtler, more nuanced; insights that have only reinforced my desire to continue with experiments that further my understanding of what Immersive Theatre 'does'.

Notes

1 The questionnaire responses received vis-à-vis the themes and intentions of the performances were the most subjective in how they were coded. It is for this reason that these responses are provided in detail within the endnotes, whereas responses to other questions are summarized and presented within the body of the chapter.
2 "What, according to you, were the main themes of the performance?"
3 Immersive Performance Spectator Responses:

Refugees/asylum seekers
Spectator A: "Refugee crisis; discrimination against immigrants."
Spectator C: "Problems in the immigration office, specifically for people who are seeking asylum" and "unfair and inhuman treatment of the asylum seekers."
Spectator E: "Problems faced by immigrants."
Spectator F: "Difficulty and struggle for refugees and people who are threaten(ed) back home to immigrate to the other country."
Spectator H: "Main themes of the performance were about the audience [who] became the refugees who seek for asylum in other country with a help of lawyer to support the case."
Spectator I: "Throughout the performance, it seemed like a major theme was the struggle of immigrants/refugees. Family and the separation of mother from child was also a component."
Spectator K: "The struggles of asylum seekers & their almost inevitable fate."

4　Immersive Performance Spectator Responses:

Systems & process of immigration
Spectator A: "The US immigration system and its flaws."
Spectator B: "Immigration and the human rights violations involved" and "The injustices of immigration processes and systems."
Spectator C: "Discrimination and lack of transparency of the process."

5　Immersive Performance Spectator Responses:

More abstract concepts
Spectator D: "Some important themes that stood out to me were pressing issues we face today like people seeking peace and being denied that."
Spectator E: "Power relations between officers, immigrants, lawyers etc."
Spectator G: "There were definite themes of oppression, hardship & drama in this piece, in my eyes."
Spectator I: "Further, it appeared to be a social commentary on the dangers of journalism in certain countries."
Spectator J: "Introduce how that people work as usual" and "To let people become part of the show" and "Use different way to act theatre."
Spectator K: "Anticipation" and "Frustration" and "Fear."

6　Proscenium Performance Spectator Responses:

Refugees/asylum seekers
Spectator A: "The main theme of the performance was refugee rights and the way they are treated when entering a new country."
Spectator C: "Refugees situation" and "How refugees are treated in the refugees camps" and "Emotions/feelings of the refugees."
Spectator E: "Asylum seeking, refugees and the process/experience they have to go through to get asylum."
Spectator F: "The brutality experienced by refugees in foreign countries."
Spectator G: "Refugee/immigration crisis."
Spectator H: "Refugee crisis."
Spectator J: "The mistreatment of asylum/refugee seekers."
Spectator K: "To look at the harshness displayed against refugees within detention centers."
Spectator L: "Human rights [and] immigration."
Systems & process of immigration
Spectator A: "It also commented on the topics of authorities and their way of exhibiting power."
Spectator B: "The immigration/refugee system."
Spectator F: "The backwardness of the current immigration policy employed by many countries."
Spectator H: "The System (not power)."
Spectator I: "Cheating the system?"
More abstract concepts
Spectator B: "Power & powerlessness" and "Oppression based on gender/race/age" and "Truth & stories – was she telling the truth, did it matter?" And "The passing of time."

Spectator D: "How innocence does not matter in the face of a higher authority. The higher authority holds power, no matter how unfair and whether their authority is made up or not by themselves" and "some individuals interpret their roles in society into ones of power and take any power that they can to exercise control over other individuals."

Spectator E: "Fairness/unfairness of believing one's story" and "The desperation of not knowing what will happen and what to do to get what you want. The hope of having a better future."

Spectator G: "Emotions of desperation, exhaustion, sympathy" and "Emotional abuse."

Spectator H: "Female/femininity" and "lying" and "religion" and "pain."

Spectator I: "War?"

Spectator J: "Violence, emotional trauma, and the theme of honesty/truth."

Spectator L: "Gender equality."

7 "What, according to you, were the intentions of the creators, i.e., what were they intending to evoke from the audience?"

8 Proscenium Performance Spectator Responses

Feeling-based responses

Spectator B: "I think they wanted us to feel what it was like to go through the refugee process. I think they wanted us to be able to attach a personal story to this issue."

Spectator E: "A sense of solidarity, empathy towards the main character and what she was going through, feel the [. . .] and frustration that one might feel in those circumstances."

Spectator F: "Intended to evoke sympathy from the audience regarding the treatment that refugees/asylum seekers have to go through."

Spectator G: "Sympathy/empathy."

Non-feeling-based responses

Spectator A: "I think the creators wanted the audience to get a new perspective on the refugee crises and to open their minds to understanding not only refugees harsh background but also how challenging it is to arrive in a new country."

Spectator C: "Show people how's the refugees situation and how they are treated."

Spectator D: "Trying to make the audience pick a side that of the young woman or that of the interrogators, prison guard and people that didn't believe her."

Spectator E: "Also, to communicate in detail about personal experience [. . .] and raise awareness."

Spectator F: "Make the audience more aware about the conditions that some people are subjected to."

Spectator H: "Sympathy for both sides of the argument (asylum seekers/ lawyers/ guards/ government official)."

Spectator I: "Remind us, as to how brutal the imprisonment system in the U.S. is. Well not the prison system, I don't know what the right term would be, but I hope you know what I mean."

Spectator J: "I think that the intentions of the creators were to inform and expose the audience into the situations those refugees were in. I also think that the intention was also to show the perspective of the immigration official and how difficult it is for them to make decisions based on the stories they hear and to decide whether it is real."

Spectator K: "The creator was trying to show the inhumane treatment of for-eigners/refugees that arrive undocumented to a country and are not given their rights. I believe that creator was trying to evoke sympathy for the main character, as well as show the harsh reality that those people undergo in a detention center."

Spectator L: "A sense of solidarity towards the immigrant on the play."

9 Immersive Performance Spectator Responses:

Feeling-based responses

Spectator A: "They wanted to make me feel like the character I was supposed to be, to make me feel the way like many immigrants feel every day at the immigration offices. I felt uncomfortable, hungry, frustrated, sad and afraid."

Spectator B: "I believe that the creators were trying to get the audience to further empathize with refugees, the refugee crisis, and to recognize the hardships and injustices that refugees face."

Spectator C: "Sympathy for those people seeking asylum" and "feeling of unjust treatment and inhumane treatment to the asylum seekers by the immigration officers."

Spectator D: "Fear & Sympathy."

Spectator F: "I think what they were trying to evoke was the emotions and attitude."

Spectator G: "I think the piece tried to evoke feelings of sacredness from author-ity which made us self-regulate our behaviour. A sense of helplessness, lonel[y]ness & hunger I think were also trying to be evoked. It was a very shocking & slightly degrading experience as we were moving around like cattle, being told what to do & never told why."

Spectator H: "In my opinion, the intentions were to make the audience feel uncomfortable in a certain way in this case by making audience to interact with the performers in a controlled situation."

Spectator I: "From my perspective, I think the creators were trying to evoke outrage as well as fear."

Spectator J: "Make audience feel they are part of the show then they can bet-ter to feel the acting and let themselves push the performance going up."

Spectator K: "They were trying to evoke empathy towards individuals fleeing from their countries. In addition to exploring the somewhat 'sterile' & emo-tionless way in which they are treated at the borders."

Non-feeling-based responses

Spectator F: "I think how people act under the pressure has been observed."

Spectator I: "I think they wanted to raise awareness amongst audience mem-bers in regards to the struggle of refugees. Especially after what happened recently in [the College] community with our Italian alum [who was killed in Egypt] the piece was extra potent."

10 "What is one element from the play – a scene, a technique, a character – that you found most powerful? Why?"

11 "In the role you were given during the performance – of a journalist who was facing threats in their home country – did you believe the story to be true, i.e., that the facts of the story as shared with you by the Immigration Official and the Lawyer warranted the person (you) being given asylum in the new country? Why/Why not?"

12 Rank the statements below from most to least relevant in the blanks provided. The statement that is most relevant to the performance you watched should be ranked 1 and the statement that is least relevant should be ranked 4:

- Empathy for refugees is what is most important in addressing the current global refugee crisis ____
- Activism for refugees' rights is what is most important in addressing the current global refugee crisis ____
- Information about refugees' situations is what is most important in addressing the current global refugee crisis ____
- Immigration policy reform is what is most important in addressing the current global refugee crisis ____

13 "Which character in the performance did you most identify with i.e., which character said/did something to remind you of a personal memory? Please describe what the character said/did. If you did not identify with any particular character, please leave this section blank."

14 Responses included:

Spectator C: "The asylum seekers (we, the audience) because we had to make sure we followed the rules, stood in line and listened to instruct[ions], had to dress nicely in order to convince the official, and had to make sure everything was perfect in order to get the change to enter the country or defend why we want and deserve to be here."

Spectator D: "The lady with a family she had to leave behind, because many times I've had to see family members leave what they were comfortable for better education even though it was by choice it's still a sad thing they have to leave what the[y] love and who they love behind"

Spectator C: "The [Waiting Room] officer who was trying to be nice to us and also emphasize with his boss. Reminded me of times when I was working and felt a bit in the same situation."

Spectator F: "Officer. When I came to the US I needed to get visa. At that time I wasn't able to speak English at all. That officer was kind of similar to the Officer I saw yesterday."

Spectator G: "When I was sitting for my interview & [the Officer] was being very in my face, confident & rude I experienced the same feeling of helplessness when I got in trouble at school and couldn't say the real story & had to just push the only information I had even though I knew it wouldn't be enough to help my situation."

Spectator H: "The scene when the other refugee [. . .] when she get kicked out by [the Officer] really violently."

Spectator G: "On a much more toned-down level, I related a bit with [the Fellow Detainee], only because my dad moved to the US when I was 2 months old and my mom and I didn't join him until I was 8 years old. My family is pretty familiar with the nuances of immigration but our situation was definitely nowhere near as dire."

15 Three men went all the way to 450 volts, and seventeen broke off despite being urged to continue.

16 The front page of each journal had this note on it:

Please make notes in the journal as and when you recall the performance over the next month. If you can, please note the following:

- The date on which you make the entry
- The stimulus that made you recall the performance
- The specific aspect of the performance that you remembered
- The thoughts and/or emotions evoked by the memory of the performance.

The questions above are simply prompts to guide your entries. Please feel free to craft your own questions or write in an unstructured fashion – whatever works best for you! The journal will need to be handed in when you come to your interview.

Works cited

Bernsten, D. & Rubin, D. C. 2012. *Understanding Autobiographical Memory: Theories and Approaches.* New York: Cambridge University Press.

Biggin, R. 2015. Reading fan mail: Communicating immersive experience in Punchdrunk's *Faust* and *The Masque of the Red Death. Participations: Journal of Audience & Reception Studies.* 12(1):301–317.

Corcoran, K. J. 1982. Behavioral and nonbehavioral methods of developing two types of empathy: A comparative study. *Journal of Education for Social Work.* 18(3):85–93.

Helms, N. R. 2012. Upon such sacrifices: An ethic of spectator risk. *Journal of Dramatic Theory and Criticism.* 27(1):91–107.

Keen, S. 2006. A theory of narrative empathy. *Narrative.* 14(3):207–236.

Koriat, A. & Melkman, R. 1987. Depth of processing and memory organization. *Psychological Research.* 49:173–181.

McConachie, B. 2008. *Engaging Audiences: A Cognitive Approach to Spectating in the Theatre.* Basingstoke and New York: Palgrave Macmillan.

Perry, G. 2013. *Behind the Shock Machine: The Untold Story of the Notorious Milgram Psychology Experiments.* New York and London: New Press.

Reason, M. & Reynolds, D. 2010. Kinesthesia, empathy, and related pleasures: An inquiry into audience experiences of watching dance. *Dance Research Journal.* 42(2):49–75.

Reisberg, D. & Heuer, F. 1992. Remembering the details of emotional events. *Affect and Accuracy in Recall: Studies of "Flashbulb" Memories.* E. Winograd & U. Neisser (Eds). Cambridge: Cambridge University Press. 162–190.

Rotgans, J. I. & Schmidt, H. G. 2014. Situational interest and learning: Thirst for knowledge. *Learning and Instruction.* 32:37–50.

Tobias, S. 1994. Interest, prior knowledge, and learning. *Review of Educational Research.* 64(1):37–54.

Zimbardo, P. 2007. *The Lucifer Effect: Understanding How Good People Turn Evil.* New York: Random House.

4 The data and the actors

Memo #7

I have had actors in both proscenium and immersive performances comment on the power of the theatrical process. But it
was only in my first Immersive Theatre project as a director (the
project from Kashmir that I described earlier) where I encountered the relative power that an actor in an immersive experience
has. In a proscenium piece, the director watches the show from
afar, and I have seen one performance in which a director was
so unhappy with what was happening on stage that she inter-
rupted the show and asked her actors to start the show from the
top. I have also seen directors in proscenium performances give
extensive feedback to their actors after each show, thus exhibiting their (potential) control over subsequent performances. Of
course, actors can still do as they please when they are on stage
and the director remains relatively powerless when compared to
the rehearsal room and yet, it is a different kind of powerlessness
that is experienced during an Immersive Theatre piece.
  In an Immersive Theatre piece,

> There is no way for the director to give feedback to the actors
> unless the group's resources allow each performance to
> be recorded/live streamed to the director – resources that
> I have never had. Even though I asked actors in this pro-
> ject to switch on recording devices in their interrogation
> rooms, the devices would often run out of memory during
> the middle of the performance. Or the actors would forget
> to turn on the camera in their room. Or they would not be
> able to transfer the video in time for me to view before the
> following rehearsal/show.

In an Immersive Theatre piece,

> It is difficult to know if anything goes awry backstage. For example, in one of the final rehearsals for this project – for a small invited audience that functioned as a trial for the performers – I was informed *after* the show that one of the performers (playing the role of an Interrogator) had not shown up! As a result, an actor playing the Lawyer in another scenario stood in for the absent Interrogator, during breaks that he had within his own performance. While I would have known about the issue as it unfolded in a more traditional set up, in the immersive performance, I did not know about the actor's absence until after the rehearsal was over.

In an Immersive Theatre piece,

> Actors have all the control. For example, I found out in an interview with one audience member about particular things that the actor playing the Lawyer in her scene had done – choices that the actor had *not* run past me during rehearsals; choices that I was not aware of; choices that I only came to know of after the performance. While the choices, in this case, did not significantly or negatively impact the trajectory of the scene, the extent of improvisation that is required from the actor in such immersive experiences makes it near-impossible for the director to exercise more rigorous quality checks – or maybe it's just me who has this issue?

The actor in an immersive piece and the actor in a proscenium piece require different kinds of training; different kinds of in-the-moment response strategies; different attitudes (possibly) toward the performance.

What does Immersive Theatre 'do' differently for its performers?

Going into this project my primary goal was to compare the responses between two spectator groups. However, in the midst of the rehearsal process – upon observing the ways in which the two groups of performers were engaging with their work – I also decided to institute a feedback mechanism for the performers and consider differences in the actors' modes of engagement. This late realization led to two limitations: the first is that I was unable to ask the performers to keep process journals during the rehearsals – process journals that might have been an incredibly useful tool in addition to the post-performance mechanisms that were instituted. The second limitation lies in the difference between the numbers of performers in each performance. While it initially did not bother me that there were only five actors in the proscenium piece in comparison with the twenty performers in the immersive piece, this difference became a point of consideration when I decided to analyze actors' feedback. The greater number of respondents in the immersive group led to more robust data being available, while there was relatively far less data available from the five proscenium actors. While I am cognizant of these limitations, I still think that considering feedback from the actors provides some thought-provoking avenues to pursue. Furthermore, what becomes particularly interesting is placing the data from the actors in conversation with what was revealed by the spectators. Are there ways in which the data from the spectators and the data from the actors resonate with/fracture from each other? What might the similarities/differences across the actor and spectator groups imply for the use of Immersive Theatre as a form? Like the previous chapter, this one is also structured around sections that contain the data that emerged from each of the four different feedback mechanisms: the questionnaires, the focus group discussions, the individual interviews, and the journal entries. Each section includes an overview of the data that emerged, a brief discussion of my analyses of these emergences, and a comparison (where useful) with the corresponding data from the spectators. A summary of my highlights from these pieces of data and their analyses is elaborated upon at the end of the chapter.[1]

Data and the questionnaires

A day after the performance

In response to the question about the *themes*[2] of the performances, responses were coded using the same categorization that was employed for the spectators: responses that spoke to themes about refugees/asylum seekers, responses that had to do with themes about immigration from a policy/government standpoint, and more abstract responses that mentioned emotions that had been evoked without necessarily linking these emotions to particular concepts of characters. In so doing, I found that a larger number of the immersive actors said that their performance had themes that had to do with refugees or asylum seeking: "Confusion of what to do next as a refugee, of what is correct, what can be said, and what can't" (Immersive Performance Actor A, Questionnaire, February 2016), "Global refugee situation crisis"

(Immersive Performance Actor B, Questionnaire, February 2016), and "What is true and what is not in the stories that refugees and migrants have to tell" (Immersive Performance Actor C, Questionnaire, February 2016), for example.[3] Other responses mentioned themes related to the systems and processes of immigration: "Immigration office waiting room" (Immersive Performance Actor A, Questionnaire, February 2016), "Discrimination towards refugees by officials" (Immersive Performance Actor C, Questionnaire, February 2016), and "Legal processes" (Immersive Performance Actor E, Questionnaire, February 2016).[4] The responses also included more abstract concepts like: "Audience participation" (Immersive Performance Actor A, Questionnaire, February 2016), "Faith, Hope, Authority, Power" (Immersive Performance Actor B, Questionnaire, February 2016), "Love" (Immersive Performance Actor C, Questionnaire, February 2016), and "Empathy, Integration, Fear" (Immersive Performance Actor D, Questionnaire, February 2016).[5] Contrastingly, all five of the proscenium actors who watched the immersive performance indicated a preference for more abstract themes than those that dealt with refugees and/or policies directly.[6]

In comparison, when looking at responses vis-à-vis interpretations of the themes in the proscenium performance, it must be mentioned that six of the Immersive Theatre actors did not watch the proscenium performance. Of those that did, the thematic analyses included more responses that were related to questions surrounding refugees/asylum seekers and abstract themes, compared to themes about the systems and processes of immigration.[7] Equal number of proscenium actors thought their own performance had to do with "systems" (Proscenium Performance Actor B, Questionnaire, February 2016) as with "asylum seeker experiences" (Proscenium Performance Actor C, Questionnaire, February 2016) as with abstract concepts like "deception, manipulation" (Proscenium Performance Actor D, Questionnaire, February 2016) or "truth" (Proscenium Performance Actor E, Questionnaire, February 2016).[8] The analysis of the thematic responses from the actors alone did not seem to reveal any particular differences that are worth exploring.

When looking at responses about theme from across the actors and spectator groups though, it is interesting to note the following:

- The largest number of responses from the immersive actors indicate that their performance contained themes to do with refugees or asylum seeking.
- A majority of the proscenium actors thought that the immersive performance dealt with more abstract themes.
- Most of the spectators to the immersive performance commented that the performance's themes had to do with refugees and asylum seekers.

Looking at these three outcomes then, what seems to be given relatively less importance vis-à-vis the immersive performance is themes related to the system, i.e., to the government and/or policies surrounding immigration. This presents a contrast with the proscenium performance where:

- The actors from the immersive performance thought the piece dealt as much with themes of asylum seekers/refugees as with more abstract concepts.
- A similar number of proscenium actors thought their own performance had to do with larger systems of power as with "asylum seeker experiences" (Proscenium Performance Actor A, Questionnaire, February 2016) or with abstract concepts like "deception, manipulation" (Proscenium Performance Actor B, Questionnaire, February 2016), or "truth" (Proscenium Performance Actor C, Questionnaire, February 2016).
- While most of the spectators to the proscenium performance also commented on themes related to refugee/asylum seeking in their performance, many also spoke to themes related to the 'system', as it were, and a large number of responses also mentioned more abstract concepts and themes.

Although looking at the numbers behind each response does not immediately indicate any certainty – given the interpretive nature of coding responses and the difference in the number of actors in the two pieces – there does seem to be a notable difference in how the system or policies are seen as being more important to the proscenium rather than the immersive performance. This goes back to a possible difference between the kinds of empathy/awareness that is evoked in each of the pieces.

In looking for categories that would be useful to code responses of the second question about *intention*,[9] I invoked the same categories that were used for the spectators: responses that mentioned empathy, sympathy, or an emotion-focused intention and were coded as feeling-based responses; and responses that were coded as non-feeling-based (raising awareness was a popular one in this category). A significant majority of the actors in the immersive performance said that their piece had to do with evoking 'feelings' of some nature for asylum seekers, rather than generating awareness about the issue or providing information;[10] similarly, a larger number of the proscenium actors also thought that the intentions of the immersive performance were to heighten emotional responses.[11] In terms of the proscenium performance, a majority of the actors from the immersive performance (though less of a majority than about their own performance) said that the proscenium performance shared the same feeling-based intentions as their own work. However, a large number of these respondents also saw the proscenium performance as provoking more non-feeling-based responses compared to their own piece.[12] Similar numbers of proscenium actors said that their intention of their performance was to create feeling-based as non-feeling-based responses.[13] The intentions of the immersive performance, therefore, were seen (more often) as being hinged on provoking particular kinds of emotions or feelings, while the proscenium performance was seen (more often) as including feeling and non-feeling-based intentions.

In looking at the responses about intention across actor and spectator groups then:

- A majority of the immersive actors said that their own performance intended to evoke feeling-based responses.
- A majority of the proscenium actors shared this emphasis on feeling-based responses about their immersive counterparts' piece.
- From the spectators though, in addition to multiple feeling-based responses, many of the audience members spoke to the immersive piece's intentions of provoking 'negative'/uncomfortable sentiments (also feeling-based in their own right).

This overwhelming presence of feeling-based responses was more balanced with non-feeling-based responses in all respondent groups' interpretations of the intentions of the proscenium performance.

When asked to mention *one element* that they found to be most interesting and powerful in the performances,[14] there were small differences in what the immersive actors found to be most interesting in their own performance. Some mentioned particular strategies employed for the Immersive Theatre aesthetic, others mentioned particular scenes, moments, and characters that they found to be most interesting, and others mentioned a more holistic appreciation of their performance. A larger number of the proscenium actors mentioned finding particular immersive strategies to be most interesting in the other performance, rather than specific scenes or characters. In comparison, with regards to the proscenium performance, the immersive actors indicated a clear majority in deeming the transitions between the scenes as being the most interesting element while three of the five proscenium actors mentioned the transitions and two mentioned specific scenes from the piece. Looking at the data from actors and spectators also reveals the consistent presence of the transitions as being the most interesting element of the proscenium performance, whereas there was more diversity in what actors and audiences found to be interesting in the immersive performance.

In the next question, actors were asked to choose how they were *affected* by the performance that they watched and acted in.[15] As a result of their own performance, the immersive actors' most popular response (in some form, i.e., in isolation or combination with other responses) was (a) "I am better informed about the experiences of refugees and asylum seekers"; similarly, three of the five proscenium performers said they were better informed about the experiences of refugees and asylum seekers. Interestingly, while four of the five proscenium actors maintained the same response (a) about their own performance, the most popular response of the immersive actors about the proscenium show was (b): "I encountered an interesting story" – just as the spectators to the proscenium performance. There was an obvious trend in the responses that actors and spectators saw the immersive performance as enabling better informed spectators while they saw the proscenium performance as being centred on storytelling.

In the question about the *authenticity* of the story of the Young Woman in the proscenium piece and the refugee-audience member in the immersive piece,[16] there were equal numbers of immersive actors who believed and did not believe the story of the audience member in the immersive performance; these responses were closely followed by those who were unsure of the veracity of the audience member's story. However, there were no unsure responses about the immersive performance's authenticity from the proscenium performers: three proscenium actors did not believe the story; two of them did. In contrast, with the proscenium performance, the immersive actors were much more certain that the story of the Young Woman was true (compared to the same story of the audience member in the immersive performance); actors in the proscenium performance seemed just as likely to *not* believe the Young Woman as they were to be unsure of the authenticity of her story. Looking at the spectators and actors data did not seem to reveal any particular trends – both performances seemed to generate a similar amount of lack of certainty vis-à-vis the veracity of the protagonists' story.

Actors were asked if there was something that they did/did not *identify* with about the character that they played in their respective performances. In either case, they were asked to explain the reasons behind their responses. Almost all the actors in the immersive performance said that there was indeed something about their character that they identified with, while only two of the five proscenium actors said they did identify with some element of their characters (the actors playing the Detention Centre Guard, the Immigration Official, and the Young Woman said there was nothing about their characters that they identified with). Similarly, a large number of immersive actors said that there was something about their character that they did not/could not identify with; four proscenium actors described particularly not identifying with their characters in the performance. Although the difference between the numbers of actors in the two performances becomes a limiting factor here, these responses do seem to point toward an interesting possibility that could use further investigation. Since actors in an immersive experience, like the one in this performance, need to be ready to improvise in the moment based on their audience member's responses, is it more likely that they will look harder to find elements of their characters that they identify with irrespective of whether the characters are protagonists or antagonists? Does a proscenium, script-based performance, allow more opportunities for performers to distance themselves from the characters that they embody, especially if the characters are antagonists? And if in fact immersive performers are more likely to draw on their own autobiographical memories to aid in their characterization, what implications might this likelihood have for how these actors are trained?

Next on the questionnaire actors were asked to rank a series of statements that were aimed to gain an insight into the real-world *outcomes* that they saw as being important in addressing the global refugee crisis: *Empathy, Information, Activism*, or *Policy Reform*.[17] In speaking about their own performance, more actors in the immersive piece thought that *Information* is most relevant to addressing the global refugee crisis (in line with the effect of being better informed that was mentioned in response to the previous question); *Activism* was most often seen as being the least relevant. More proscenium actors listed *Empathy* as being most relevant to the immersive performance, while *Activism* and *Policy Reform* were most often mentioned as the least relevant and *Information* was never mentioned as being least relevant. In speaking about the proscenium performance, actors in the immersive performance chose *Empathy* and *Policy Reform* equally often as being the most relevant – while *Information* was never chosen as the first option. *Information* and *Activism* were, in fact, most often seen as being least relevant. While, as a result of their own performance, proscenium actors mostly mentioned *Empathy* as being most relevant (just as in the immersive performance), *Policy Reform* and *Empathy* were never mentioned as being least relevant.

In looking across responses from actors and spectators, there are some interesting trends that emerge. With regards to the immersive performance:

- *Information* was most relevant to the actors in the piece.
- *Empathy* was the most relevant to the proscenium actors who watched the piece.
- *Policy Reform* was seen as being most relevant to the spectators to the immersive performance.

Reflecting a similar diversity:

- Actors in the immersive performance thought that *Activism* was least relevant to their performance.
- Actors in the proscenium performance thought *Activism* and *Policy Reform* were least relevant.
- The immersive performance's spectators thought *Information* was least relevant.

Thus, there were glaring differences in each of the three groups' thoughts on this question, and I have to wonder if the *absence* of consistency across the three groups might be further evidence of the subjective nature of the immersive experience. I say this since the data from the proscenium performance reflects a different picture:

- Actors from the immersive performance chose *Empathy* and *Policy Reform* equally often as being the most relevant for the proscenium show.
- Actors from the proscenium piece mostly mentioned *Empathy* as being most relevant to their performance.
- Spectators to the proscenium show also chose *Empathy* and *Policy Reform* as being most relevant in addressing the global refugee crisis.

Exhibiting a similar pattern in what was least relevant, actors from the immersive performance saw *Information* and *Activism* as being least relevant to the proscenium piece as did both the proscenium actors themselves and their spectator group. There was significantly less variation in responses to this question vis-à-vis the proscenium performance, and this lack of variation might indicate that, when theatre makers seek to heighten subjectivity, we might want to use immersive aesthetics. However, when the desire might be to generate more 'uniform' real-world applications of what is shared in a performance, perhaps a more conventional form might be the better strategy?

Data and the group discussions

A day after the performance

Similar to the discussions that took place with the spectators, after a brief introduction about the format that the discussion would take, the floor was left open to the actors, i.e., they could choose to discuss whatever they wished to in relation to the performance. Like the spectators to the immersive performance who began by wanting to know more about their peers' experiences, the group discussion with the immersive performance's actors also began with one of the performers asking the question: "How passive or active were audience members?" (Immersive Performance Actor A, Group Discussion, February 2016). This particular actor was a Waiting Room Guard and had thus witnessed something very different than the Interrogators, Lawyers, and Fellow Detainees. This first question stimulated an extensive sharing of anecdotal information, with actors trading details about what they had observed about their audience members and about their own responses (as performers) in the privacy and intimacy of each of their scenarios. This discussion was followed by the same actor (who played a Waiting Room Guard) asking about differences that the actors might have observed between the first and second audience members who came into their scenario, i.e., if a longer stay in the waiting room had led to observable differences in how audience members interacted with actors. Once again this question provoked a sharing of anecdotes from the different actors, and later into this discussion some of the actors expressed a desire in wanting to perform the piece again. "I would love to find a way to make this bigger and take it outside" (Immersive Performance Actor F, Group Discussion, February 2016), an actor said, while a few others spoke to how the piece had contributed to their growth as performers. At this point, since the actors had brought up the notion of performing again, I asked them which performance (the immersive or the proscenium) they thought would be better shared outside the College community – building off of what the proscenium spectators had brought up in their discussion – and while one actor mentioned that the other (proscenium) performance had affected her more, it seemed to be that a larger number of actors who wanted the piece to be performed again wanted it to be their immersive adaptation.

With the actors from the proscenium piece the group discussion began with one of the actors asking the others "what [they thought] the point of the play was" (Proscenium Performance Actor A, Group Discussion, February 2016). One of the actors summarized the difference in his responses to the two different performances by saying: "This one would push me to change the policies, the immersive one would push me to donate food for them" (Proscenium Performance Actor B, Group Discussion, February 2016). Following this discussion about intention, comparisons between the immersive and proscenium performance ensued and after a time, I intervened to pose the same question as I had with the immersive actors, i.e., which of the two performance would be most appropriate to take outside the College community. There was some back and forth about this, with varied opinions that intersected with anecdotes of actors' personal encounters with visa processes, since many of them were international students studying in the United States. When there seemed to be no consensus that emerged in response to this question, one of the actors asked the group about how they had responded to the question regarding identification in the questionnaire. In response, it was only the actor who played the character of the Lawyer who admitted to identifying, in some way, with the character that she took on. None of the other actors, not even the Young Woman, shared this opinion – an occurrence that was quite different from what emerged with the actors in the immersive adaptation.

The identification between actor and character in the two aesthetics, therefore, seems to be a concept that requires more attention. Since immersive actors are required to respond to unexpected audience reactions, is it necessary for these performers to find ways of identifying with their character so as to achieve a more holistic 'personality'? This is to say, is it more necessary for the actor/character blend – from the point of view of the Immersive Theatre performer – to be more heavily underlined during the rehearsal processes? Whereas this type of identification might not be as necessary within a script-based aesthetic, where the actor is not called upon to make the same kinds of in-the-moment responses to audience reactions?

Data, the individual interviews, and the journal entries

A month after the performance

When asking actors what they remembered most about their rehearsal process, a large number of performers in the immersive piece mentioned the characterization exercises that they had undertaken through filling out character questionnaires in an early rehearsal – an exercise that I explained in Chapter 2. When asked about what they remembered most from the performances, many actors spoke about the transformation that had occurred from "the empty chair" rehearsals (Immersive Performance Actor B, Individual Interview, March 2016) – as one performer referred to the sessions in which there was no audience member present – to the sessions during which they had spectator-participants. In addition to what the actors remembered from the rehearsals and performances, an interesting consideration that emerged indicated multiple instances of actors judging the actions of their spectator-participants, i.e., whether or not a particular audience member's participation was 'good', based on how responsive they were in the interrogation rooms. This propensity for judgement is one that troubles me since, if immersive environments create problematic scenarios where actors more critically evaluate/judge their audience members, there might arise serious ethical implications for the use of the form in Applied Theatre contexts. Not to mention that when such a judgement intersects with a pre-existing relationship between actors and spectators, many more complexities emerge.

Adding to this troubling concept of judgement, two more interesting aspects emerged when talking about the actors' process of making entries in their journals. The first was a question that was posed by one performer in the Immersive Theatre piece, who asked me if there are specific kinds of actor training that might need to be implemented with performers in an immersive piece. Given the proliferation of immersive and one-to-one performances that occur in today's theatrical arena, is it time for the form's practitioners to systematize how performers are trained to partake in such an aesthetic? In addition to this question around training, listening to the immersive performance's actors speak about their process of making journal entries also revealed that twelve out of the sixteen actors who attended the interviews saw a link between their recall of the project and their experiences during Project Week. This link could be seen as the Project Week functioning as a potential real-world application of ideas they had explored through their work on the immersive performance; it also could be that the time frame in which the Project Week happened – a week after the performance – made it the right span of time for events during that week to act as stimuli for actors and spectators alike.[18] Ten out of the sixteen immersive actors who came to individual interviews made entries in their journal and there were thirty-two entries in total. Like the spectators, the largest numbers of entries were made in the first two weeks following the performance (seventeen out of twenty-eight). In a closer analysis of content in the journals, eighteen out of the twenty-eight entries mentioned direct stimuli that reminded them of the project: news reports and discussions about immigration issues in class/with peers, for instance; nine out of the twenty-eight entries mentioned more indirect stimuli; and five of the entries had unclear stimuli (see Table 4.1).

Table 4.1 Overview of immersive actors' journal entries

Actor	Stimuli
A	1. News report about refugees **[DIRECT]**
	2. Travel across US-Mexico border **[DIRECT]**
	3. Movie about immigration **[DIRECT]**
	4. Travel across the border **[DIRECT]**
	5. Personal reaction to an event at school **[INDIRECT]**
B	1. Journal itself **[DIRECT]**
	2. Segregation in Project Week location **[INDIRECT]**
	3. **[UNCLEAR]** stimulus
	4. Personal visa issue **[DIRECT]**
C	1. **[UNCLEAR]**
D	1. Travel back from Mexico and Film Festival **[DIRECT]**
E	1. Travel across the border **[DIRECT]**
F	1. **[UNCLEAR]** stimulus
	2. UN visit **[DIRECT]**
	3. Own theatre performance **[INDIRECT]**
	4. **[UNCLEAR]** stimulus
G	1. Travel **[INDIRECT]**
	2. Saying goodbye to a loved one **[INDIRECT]**
	3. Seeing diversity on campus **[INDIRECT]**

(Continued)

Table 4.1 (Continued)

Actor	Stimuli
H	1. Crossing the US-Mexico border **[DIRECT]** 2. Movie about immigration **[DIRECT]** 3. Movie about immigration **[DIRECT]** 4. Travel across the border **[DIRECT]** 5. Class discussion about immigration **[DIRECT]**
I	1. Travel **[INDIRECT]** 2. UN flags on a visit during Project Week **[INDIRECT]** 3. A specific place on Project Week **[INDIRECT]** 4. Meeting an immigrant on Project Week **[DIRECT]** 5. **[UNCLEAR]** stimulus 6. Class discussion about immigration **[DIRECT]**
J	1. Conversation with theatre student about the performance **[DIRECT]** 2. The journal itself **[DIRECT]**

Six out of the sixteen immersive actors who came to the individual interviews did not make any entries.

In comparison with the immersive performance's actors, only three of the five actors in the proscenium piece attended the individual interviews. When asked about what they remembered about the rehearsal process, all three individuals mentioned recalling elements related to the characterization of their roles – the struggles and challenges of that process. When asked about what they remembered about the performance, while some general comments were made about the improvements the performers witnessed between the rehearsals and the final performance, the actor playing the Young Woman brought up the same question as a spectator to the immersive performance: the impact of knowing one's audience members and how prior knowledge of one's spectators might impact an (amateur) actor's performances. Following these questions about what the performers remembered about their rehearsals and performances, when we discussed the journal entries, two of the three actors mentioned not having made any notes at all. One of these actors mentioned no recall occurred for her despite having read news stories about refugees in the intervening month. The other actor who had not made any journal entries – apart from a one-line entry in which he said he had thought of the performance when he saw the journal laying on his desk – was himself a refugee from Syria and had participated in a Project Week expedition that dealt with juvenile incarceration and justice. Yet, despite this lived experience of events/themes addressed in *The Bogus Woman,* this actor mentioned not having recalled the performances in the preceding month. The student who played the role of the Young Woman was the only actor who used the journal from the proscenium performance ensemble: six entries in total. Half of these entries took place in the week immediately after the performance, and her stimuli included four direct stimuli, one indirect stimulus, and one entry in which the provocation was unclear.[19] None of these three actors mentioned a desire to do the show again, unlike four of the performers from the immersive piece (one-fourth of those who came to the interviews) who explicitly expressed an interest in sharing their performance with more spectators from within/outside the College.

Although a more rigorous comparison of actors' responses is challenging because of the difference in the numbers of respondents in each piece, I have wondered if the actors in the immersive performance were more invested/interested in this project than their proscenium counterparts. I say this because of observable differences in the enthusiasm/interest that was displayed during the next-day discussions, the relative lack of attendance from the proscenium show's actors at the individual interviews, and the comparative dearth of journal entries from the same group of actors. If I am right in observing this difference in investment, what implications might such an occurrence have? Could varying degrees of performers' investment in a piece be a worthy avenue for further investigation? Are (amateur) actors more likely to invest in their characters/performances when they see themselves as protagonists? By extension, since more actors were protagonists in the immersive performance as compared to the proscenium piece, could this enhanced ability to be a leading character explain the difference in investment that I observed between the two groups of actors? What if the proscenium performance had also been one in which all the performers had major roles; would that have led to a marked difference in the performers' degree of engagement? And finally, how does actors' perception of novelty (of form and/or content) affect their investment in a performance?

Highlights from the data

As performers we have noticed an interesting phenomenon in terms of the way we remember traditional theatre performances versus intimate performances [. . .] Over the years we gradually realized that we remember intimate performances in significantly greater detail than theatre performances. Performances on stage go by in a bit of a blur, leaving us with only general impressions of the experience from one performance to the next. In performances to small audiences, however we retain very clear memories of the audience members, how they reacted, what they looked like, what they laughed at and when they looked thoughtful, and so we also remember ourselves and what we were doing in those moments more distinctly. We have two theories as to why this might be. The first relates to the nature of the three kinds of memory: episodic memory is remembering an event that actually happened to you; generic memory is memory of general knowledge, such as the alphabet; procedural memory is memory of skills and procedures that one has learned, like playing a musical instrument. Our personal memories (or lack thereof) suggest to us that we experience theatre performances as 'procedural' and intimate performances as 'episodic'. This implies two very different cognitive states for a performer in these two types of work: in conversational theatre we are in a skills mode, performing something we have learned in the same way the musician performs a song; in intimate performance, even though we have memorized lines and rehearsed a sequence of actions, we are engaged in an experience with the audience members and remember the event in the same cognitive manner that we process episodes in our lives. Procedural modes are by nature more automatic, a kind of autopilot made possible by rehearsal, so it doesn't seem particularly surprising that we wouldn't remember the distinct differences between performances in a run or a tour of a theatre show in great detail. – (Though if you give us the first line, we could probably repeat the entire text of any of these shows, calling on our procedural memory.)

The excerpt above, from Leslie Hill and Helen Paris's (2014:16–17) work as performers within immersive / one-to-one / intimate theatre experiences, alludes to more far-reaching cognitive implications about how the performer in a participatory/intimate aesthetic might use different ways of remembering and accessing a performance than their counterparts in a more conventional, script-based process. While my decision to include actors' feedback came too late to include a consideration of differences in their rehearsal processes, the questionnaires, discussions, individual interviews, and journal entries point toward a few concepts that might benefit from more analysis.

First, the consideration that emerges as interesting for me is how/if a more *systematic framework* might evolve for training actors in immersive performances. While Stanislavski's (1989) system has become influential for actors in Realism/Naturalism settings and Brecht's (1964) offerings are important for Dialectical/Epic efforts, I am yet to come across a more holistic systemization of training for the kind of immersive/participatory environment that was explored in this performance. I say 'this kind of' immersive performance since Augusto Boal (1985) does offer guidance for the actor in Theatre of the Oppressed, and performers like Hill and Paris have designed an *Autobiology* system for their approach to performance-making in intimate aesthetics; my own evolving ideas about this topic will be discussed in the *Memo* that ends this chapter.

The other interesting emergence was from looking at both actors' and spectators' feedback, in terms of what they deem important vis-à-vis real-world ways to address the global refugee crisis. A question that I initially used so as to assess if different outcomes were suggested by spectators to the two performance forms, considering responses to this question from the spectators alone revealed similar choices being made across both groups. However, when this data was placed in conversation with the responses from the actors, there was a *greater variety of responses* to the immersive performance as compared with the proscenium performance. In one sense this is not entirely surprising since the personalized nature of the immersive performance predicates responses that are more diverse; responses that are not only based on the personal background of the individual in question but are also influenced by the individual's familiarity with theatre. The consistency in the actors' and spectators' responses to this question in the proscenium performances, however, does seem to suggest that there was something about the form that allowed a more uniform understanding of real-world applications to emerge. This is certainly an observation that warrants further consideration.

A third point of interest emerges when reflecting upon the general sense of *increased investment* that seemed to arise from the actors in the immersive performance. These differences manifested in how the performance was spoken about, in the interest that was expressed toward performing again, and in the relatively larger number of immersive actors who came to the follow-up conversations and made journal entries. This increased investment might be explained both by the novelty of Immersive Theatre for this student demographic and by the fact that all the actors in the immersive piece were protagonists in their own right. On the contrary, the Young Woman was the only protagonist in the conventional performance and all the actors seemed unsurprised by the form of the piece, i.e., the proscenium aesthetic was not novel for them. Therefore, a combination of the form's novelty (or lack thereof) and the ability of the actors to be protagonists might have led to more excitement, interest, and/or investment for the actors in the immersive performance. Of course, this desire for novelty and for being a protagonist might also be attributes of this particular demographic: high-achieving young people who (generally) want more agency in crafting their performances and seek more experimentation with form. However, with more experienced or older actors, there might be different outcomes that are observed.

The final point to highlight from the performers' responses is the problematic way in which *audience members' participation was judged* as being 'good' or 'better' based on how much the spectator-participant spoke/interacted with the performers. Apart from the natural inclination of (young) actors to desire more interaction with their spectators and thus create unexpected scenarios during the course of an immersive experience, there are important questions around cultural codes of participation that emerge in thinking about this sort of judgement. The College demographic consists of students from over sixty countries, and this national diversity is problematized by a cultural homogeneity that emerges from having a large number of middle- and upper-middle-class students who have been educated in Anglophone contexts. Despite this cultural homogeneity though, there are still many students at the College who do not fit this 'cultural profile' and, as a result, find the ways in which they participate to be judged by others (staff and students alike) as being 'less than'. These are often the students who do not speak too often in class discussions or who do not participate vocally in student community discussions; it is often impossible to discern if this quietness stems from cultural codes that govern respect/participation or if these more quiet students are simply apathetic. Having some actors speak in judgemental terms about audience responses, therefore, leads me to wonder about this less-considered ethical dimension to participatory forms where there is a certain 'ideal spectator' that is created in the mind of the performer. Though one could argue that proscenium pieces also impose their own ideals for the spectator – of their being silent, turning off their phones, and so on – there does seem to be a different dimension that materializes when the spectators are being judged in an immersive context.

Memo #8

The highlights from the data in this chapter raise interesting questions vis-à-vis my work in places of war.

Systematizing training

In this experiment, the rehearsal process for the two groups evolved as shown in Table 4.2.

Table 4.2 Evolution of rehearsal process

Immersive Performance	Proscenium Performance
Table reading	Table reading
Characterization	Characterization
Blocking	Blocking
Adding in technical design	Adding in technical design
Final rehearsals	Final rehearsals

In thinking about the different skills that are required from each of the performance forms then, in an effort to begin a process in which training for Immersive Theatre might be systematized, it is useful to consider what particular skills are required from the actor in each of these aesthetics (in the specific ways that the forms were used in this project) (see Table 4.3).

The next step in any systemization of performer training would involve working out how each of the particular aspects mentioned here would then be nurtured/created through the use of particularly targeted and designed exercises. But that is the material for another book.

Table 4.3 Skills required of actors

Immersive Performance	Proscenium Performance
A familiarity with the context that is being simulated in the performance and an understanding of the various scenarios that create the performance.	A familiarity and comfort with the script of the performance.
A facility with improvisation that allows the actor the confidence to improvise in situ, in the face of unexpected reactions from audience members.	A knowledge and comfort with the technical cues that are relevant to the entire performance.
The creation of an ensemble between the actors in a scenario (rather than the whole performance) and a relationship with the director that enables a clear understanding of the kinds of off-book improvisations that do (not) fit within the vision for the performance.	The creation of an ensemble between all the actors, so that they might look for each other in the event of one person forgetting a line or a cue.
Creating a holistic character that is framed by the information in the script and by the context being simulated in the experience (and of course, the actor's imagination).	Creating a holistic character that is framed by the information in the script and by the context being simulated in the experience (and of course, the actor's imagination).

Subjectivity

- Conflict zones are often entrenched in binaries: good and evil, victim and perpetrator, war and peace. In such polarized contexts, can the subjectivity inspired by an Immersive Theatre piece be overwhelming and potentially risky?
- Or can subjectivity function not only as an aesthetic strategy, but also as a pedagogical one?
- Is there a way to prepare (particularly anxious/vulnerable) performers and spectators for the subjectivity that they might encounter in an immersive experience?

Increased investment

- Is novelty in an aesthetic form more likely to increase the investment of amateur actors versus more experienced performers?
- Similarly, is the size of a role – or the ability to be a protagonist – a mitigating factor for actors, based on their prior levels of experience?
- While increased investment in immersive forms might be tied to the agency it gives performers, can this agency be dangerous in a conflict zone in the event of an actor going too far with their improvised response to a spectator's reaction?

Actors' judgement of spectators

- How might the director of an immersive piece address actors' ideas of an 'ideal' spectator during the rehearsal process?
- Especially in a conflict zone, where judgements are likely to extend across community/ tribal/ ethnic/ religious/ racial lines, what checks need to be in place to ensure that spectators encounter a judgement free space?
- Are there situations where the actors' judgement of spectators' participation might actually have positive repercussions?

While I wish I had decided to include actors' experiences earlier on in this project and designed additional mechanisms to analyze their processes more rigorously – better late than never, I suppose! – there is clearly much theory-generation that can occur from considering the experiences of performers in immersive aesthetics. Theory-generation that will not only help us, as theatre practitioners and researchers, nuance our approach to immersive performances, but also hone our approach to the training that leads up to immersive performances.

With these various highlights in mind, from actors and spectators, let us move on to the Conclusions.

Notes

1 The questionnaire responses received vis-à-vis the themes and intentions of the performances were the most subjective in how they were coded. It is for this reason that these responses are provided in detail within the endnotes, whereas responses to other questions are summarized and presented within the body of the chapter.

2 What, according to you, were the main themes of the performance you watched/acted in?

3 Immersive Performance Actors (about their own performance)

Refugees/asylum seekers
Actor C: "Helplessness of refugees [and] the limited rights of refugees."
Actor D: "Refugees."
Actor F: "Confusion was definitely one of the main themes – confusion of what to do next as a refugee, of what is correct, what can be said and what can't."
Actor G: "Human migration."
Actor H: "Global refugee situation/crisis."
Actor I: "The feeling of being an unwanted, unloved alien."
Actor J: "What it is to be a foreigner in another country."
Actor F: "Refugees or immigrants situation (in any context)."
Actor L: "What is true and what is not in the stories that refugees and migrants have to tell."
Actor M: "Asylum."
Actor N: "Refugee crisis [and] illegal admission to a country."
Actor O: "Refugee assistance [and] struggle of the refugees and their confusion [and] their uncertainty of how to decide if a person needs asylum or not."
Actor R: "The main themes I felt from the play I acted would be distrust, questioning, indifference and refusal towards the refugees and the helpless situation of the refugees as well as their bitter, threatened and hard life."
Actor L: "The history of a refugee whose appeal at the end is dismissed and s/he had to come back home, even though the lawyer was doing the best to prevent this situation."
Actor S: "Let people actually feel how does it feel like to be a refugee and asks other for help."

4 Immersive Performance Actors (about their own performance)

The systems and processes of immigration
Actor J: "How a detention center works [and] immigration policy."
Actor L: "Indifference/hostility of the authorities towards migrants and refugees [and] the confusion and disorientation that a refugee can feel in the admissions process."
Actor M: "Bureaucracy, paperwork, law."
Actor N: "More exact helpfulness and effort of the immigration officers."
Actor O: "Immigration policies."

5 Immersive Performance Actors (about their own performance)

More abstract concepts
Actor E: "Intimidation [and] experiencing not just seeing/hearing."
Actor F: "Distress was another major theme."
Actor G: "New theatre [and] empathy."
Actor I: "Cruel behaviour towards victims of crime, no chance of equality, absence of all human needs: love, affection, understanding, compassion, sympathy, listening."
Actor J: "Injustice [and] power."
Actor K: "Human rights violation [and] trust/justice."
Actor M: "Emotional distress. dilemma; refugee status, family; uncertainty, fear."
Actor Q: "How it feels like to be dependent on a few stranger's decisions, confusion, fear, compassion, the difference between hearing about something and experiencing it yourself."

6 Proscenium Performance Actors (about the immersive performance)

Refugees/asylum seekers
Actor A: "Refugee's experience in foreign countries."
Actor D: "Getting used to, and being confused in, a new country."

The systems and processes of immigration
Actor B: "Immigration, bureaucracy."
Actor D: "Immigration laws."

More abstract concepts
Actor B: "Stress."
Actor C: "Inferiority, not understanding, loneliness."
Actor D: "Communication difficulties."
Actor E: "Putting yourself into the shoes of another, fear, confusion, [and] being in an environment you are unfamiliar with/don't understand."

7 Immersive Performance Actors (about the proscenium performance)

Refugees/asylum seekers
Actor B: "Immigration [and] support (refugee to refugee)."
Actor C: "The limited voice of refugees."
Actor D: "Refugees."
Actor D: "Empathy for refugees."
Actor J: "How it feels to be an immigrant in a detention center."
Actor K: "Human rights violation [and] pain or other feelings caused by refuges/immigrants situation in any situation."

Actor L: "Social and moral commentary of the so called 'grey zones' in the story of a person seeking asylum."

Actor O: "Struggle of the refugees and traumas" and "Frustration of the refugees and a feeling of powerlessness."

Actor P: "Unfairness of the immigration system towards the refugees and the anger and sorrow of the refugee. Meanwhile the[y] can't really do anything but being pushed away."

Actor Q: "Human rights."

Actor S: "How helpless refugee are in certain circumstances."

The systems and processes of immigration

Actor G: "US immigration."

Actor I: "Fight against the authorities."

Actor L: "Inhumanity of the system towards migrants and refugees."

Actor O: "Brutality in homeland security organization and lack of respect for the refugees' human rights."

More abstract concepts

Actor A: "Distress."

Actor B: "Restlessness."

Actor C: "Discrimination [and] abuse of power."

Actor D: "Fear, despair, hope, [and] hopelessness."

Actor E: "Showing all the stuff we don't see."

Actor I: "Depression [and] unbearable circumstances."

Actor J: "How easy it is to violate human rights [and] how power can be misused and abused."

Actor K: "Trust/justice."

Actor L: "Isolation and feeling of helplessness [. . .] sense of temporal suspension during a prolonged visiting."

Actor Q: "Different ways to respond to situations [of the characters and] boundaries between personal and profession and them breaking, abuse, being out of control of your own life."

8 Proscenium Performance Actors (about their own performance)

Refugees/asylum seekers

Actor A: "Refugee's experience in foreign countries."

Actor C: "Being in a foreign country, refugees' need of help."

Actor E: "The struggles of an asylum seeker" and "Insensitivity to the hardships of a foreigner."

The systems and processes of immigration

Actor B: "Immigration (not really a theme as much as a topic)."

Actor D: "Immigration laws."

Actor E: "Life inside a detention centre."

More abstract concepts

Actor B: "Justice, truth, personal suffering."

Actor B: "Loneliness."

Actor D: "Deception/manipulation [and] violence."

9 "How would you describe the intentions of the performance you watched/acted in, i.e., what were we trying to evoke from the audience?"

10   Immersive Performance Actors (about their own performance)

Feeling-based responses

Actor A: "The intention of the performance was to create a simulation of an experience. To evoke feelings from all the broad range of feelings that you can feel, being in a position of a refugee [and] mostly negative feelings: frustration, anger, helplessness."

Actor B: "Try to show the audience the situation/feelings etc. of an actual immigrant [and] evoke empathy for fellow detainee."

Actor C: "To allow the audience member to be in a position to have a first-hand experience in such a situation [and] the audience members were given a chance to feel exactly how a refugee undergoes a deportation process."

Actor E: "A personal response. Being put in the situation. Maybe anger etc."

Actor D: "It was trying to make the audience member think about what a refugee goes through when they are questioned. How they are treated, how people act around them, what people think about them. It's meant to make us think and try and relate."

Actor F: "We were trying to evoke real like emotions those of worry and confusion. The feeling of helplessness too was what the audience member was meant to feel."

Actor G: "Trigger reflection through emotion [and] empathy forced into someone."

Actor H: "Make them feel a real refugee situation [and] introduce me to this experience."

Actor I: "Unfairness, inequality, abuse/violence, [and] giving the feeling of being alone, powerless, hated and unwanted [and] feeling guilt for the situation the refugee is in."

Actor J: "Evoke hate, superiority, power, domination."

Actor K: "I think that because of the facts that it was immersive that the main intention was to make the audience members feel the implications of being a refugee."

Actor L: "Confusion, Fear, Isolation, Alienation."

Actor M: "An understanding of the more personal, human, emotional side of the process of obtaining asylum."

Actor N: "Fear from the audience and understanding of real world situation how refugees and illegal immigrants are processed."

Actor O: "For my performance, my intention was to make the audience feel confused and to make them understand the situation they were in. We (me and the other two actors in my group) tried to do it as office like as possible. It was to create frustration on the audience for having to wait so much for not knowing what was going on."

Actor P: "To let the audience experience the emotions and situation of a refugee such as anger, helplessness, sorrow, fear. Thus evoke their awareness of the refugee problem and the injustice or indifference towards the refugees."

Actor Q: "It was supposed to give the audience the chance to experience how it feels to apply for asylum including the waiting, being a number, insecurity and fear. They also got the chance to experience that their actions matter, because they could ask questions and they could have helped the fellow detainee."

Actor R: "To 'force' them to reflection about refugee situations, especially during nowadays when this topic is very present in political situation. We wanted to make this performance as reliable as it possible to make audience feel serious, to cause empathy."

Non-feeling-based responses

Actor M: "Raising the question whether the process is (un)fair and the difficulty of the hearing."

Actor N: "Helpfulness of the guards, lawyer and fellow detainee."

Actor S: "Make audience think about refugee issues."

11 Proscenium Performance Actors (about the immersive performance)

Feeling-based responses

Actor A: "A feeling that you were the one suffering of being deported."

Actor B: "Understanding of the process of immigration as well as the stress and other related feelings."

Actor C: "Make you feel how a refugee feels, make you feel like a not important thing, not a person."

Actor D: "Empathy for refugees and willingness to help them endure the harsh immigration policies and people who control the future."

Actor E: "I think the performance I watched tried to shock the audience and confuse them totally. I think that performance could have inspired more compassion, since it was immersive."

12 Immersive Performance Actors (about the proscenium performance)

Feeling-based responses

Actor A: "The feeling I felt the most was empathy. Pity, even. I felt as if the purpose of this performance is to raise awareness, educate about the experience of being a refugee through evoking feelings of guilt in the audience and feeling bad for the lead character."

Actor B: "Showing the personal experience of immigration and how a specific person lived and experienced it. Her struggles, hopes, concerns, feelings [and the] unfairness of the process of immigration."

Actor E: "Personal response, sympathy, sadness possibly. Reflection."

Actor J: "They were trying to make the audience feel empathetic with [the Young Woman] and to see a reality we are not used to. Feel what it is to be an immigrant where there is no support provided and loneliness is a huge issue."

Actor L: "Pity, Doubt, Fear, Compassion."

Actor O: "I believe the intention was also to evoke frustration in the audience. It tried to make us feel compassionate and sorry for the refugee. It was to evoke emotions from the audience by knowing what was going on but being unable to help."

Actor S: "The desperation and the injustice of everyone."

Actor I: "No escape from the miserable situation, hands are tied, [and] no one is really interested in helping the refugee. Refugee is treated like a virus that must be defeated."

Non-feeling-based responses

Actor D: "The intentions were to make you think and question the asylum seeking process. It's supposed to make want to do something and make a change."

Actor G: "Recreating a situation to inform and denounce."

Actor C: "As an audience, I could see and understand the play, showing us how it is like to be in such a situation but I lack the relatable feeling, only being a spectator."

Actor K: "As an audience member I could also feel what they were trying to transmit. However, besides feeling it, I was able to look at it from an outside perspective and therefore analyze the situation. I think that was the main intention."

Actor Q: "It was supposed to show us how asking for asylum could be like. We were supposed to feel empathy for the characters on stage but at the same time be aware that it is only a play and a metaphor for the story of million immigrants."

13 Proscenium Performance Actors (about their own performance)

Feeling-based responses

Actor B: "Sympathy for the immigrant and understanding of immigrants' lives."

Actor C: "Empathy for the young woman [and] anger for the officer/guard/foreign country."

Actor E: "I think my performance was meant to inspire empathy in the audience, and let them know about a whole world of things that are happening that they are unaware of."

Non-feeling-based responses

Actor A: "Understanding from a wise voice or someone who had already gone through what the protagonist has gone through."

Actor D: "The performance tried to evoke a wish for the way immigrants are treated to be changed [and] it is unclear whether the young woman is lying or not, but that is irrelevant to the fact that she was treated badly."

14 "What is one element from the play that you acted in/watched – a scene, a technique, a character – that you found most powerful? Why?"

15 As a result of the play that you watched/acted in, which of the following statements best describes how you have been affected (You can circle more than one response):

   a. I am better informed about the experiences of refugees and asylum seekers
   b. I encountered an interesting story
   c. I want to help refugees and asylum seekers
   d. Other:

16 Do you believe the story of the refugee audience member/the Young Woman? Why/why not?

17 Rank the statements below from most to least relevant in the blanks provided. The statement that is most relevant to the performance (that you watched and performed in) should be ranked 1 and the statement that is least relevant should be ranked 4:

- Empathy for refugees is what is most important in addressing the current global refugee crisis ____
- Activism for refugees' rights is what is most important in addressing the current global refugee crisis ____
- Information about refugees' situations is what is most important in addressing the current global refugee crisis ____
- Immigration policy reform is what is most important in addressing the current global refugee crisis ____

18 Might this indicate that month was too long a time frame within which to expect a recording of responses? Would a two-week time frame be a better control in future experiments, with this particular demographic of creators and spectators?
19 In her accounts of stimulus, she mentioned the following: (1) Skyping with family and talking about the play [DIRECT]; (2) Interacting with an audience member from the performance [DIRECT]; (3 and 4) Interacting with an audience member of the immersive performance [DIRECT]; (5) Packing bag during Project Week [INDIRECT]; (6) [UNCLEAR].

Works cited

Boal, A. 1985. *Theatre of the Oppressed.* New York: Theatre Communications Group.
Brecht, B. 1964. A short organum for the theatre. *Brecht on Theatre: Development of an Aesthetic.* J. Willett (Ed). London: Methuen.
Hill, L. & Paris, H. 2014. *Performing Proximity: Curious Intimacies.* Basingstoke: Palgrave Macmillan.
Stanislavski, C. 1989. *An Actor Prepares.* London: Routledge.

Conclusions

There are two interweaving conversations in this concluding chapter. In the first part, I revisit the performance of *Cages* (2013) that was described in Chapter 1 and think about how some of the outcomes from this experiment might apply to my work as an Applied Theatre practitioner-researcher in contexts of conflict. The second section uses these considerations toward proposing different conditions of Immersive Theatre that I seek to experiment with in future work in my theatre lab. Before embarking on this conversation, however, it is important to restate some of the highlights that emerged from spectators' and actors' responses in this experiment. As a summary of the spectators' responses, these are the following ideas that emerged as containing potential for further exploration: the *different shades of empathy* that are created in response to two different aesthetic forms; the idea that, in an immersive experience, audience members are likely to be most drawn toward *another sympathetic character* in their experience, i.e., one that references their experience in some way; that the immersive piece seemed to generate a situational *interest* whereas the proscenium piece seemed to generate more topic-focused interest; the notion of identity and the implications of having *pre-existing personal relationships* define how actors/spectators ultimately respond to each other; the implications of conceptual *processing* occurring for the immersive spectators in contrast to associative processing for the proscenium spectators. From the actors' responses there are additional concepts to add to this list: how/if a more systematic framework might evolve vis-à-vis *training actors* in immersive performances; that there was a far greater *variety in responses* in the immersive piece – to the question that sought to ascertain real-world 'solutions' to the problems being addressed in the performances – when looking at data that emerged across actor and spectator groups; that there seemed to be a general sense of *increased investment* in the immersive piece from its performers, compared to the interest demonstrated by the actors in the proscenium show; that there emerged a potentially problematic way in how audience members' participation in the immersive piece was *judged* as being 'good' or 'better' (by actors) based on how much they spoke/interacted with the performers. So, how do I take these insights with me into my work using theatre in conflict zones? In order to think about this question I revisit *Cages*, the first immersive piece that I directed that placed Kashmiri men in the shoes of women in the region. The piece asked the men to put on bridal clothes and – through an immersive journey that took them from their brother's home to the home of their in-laws – the audience member-brides were asked to undertake household chores and to participate in waiting for their husbands who have gone off to 'fight' in various ways. Audience member brides in this piece were invited to use their experience as a way to think through how gender influences the ways in which Kashmir's conflicts are engaged with (or not).

After one of the performances of *Cages* I heard a loud and heated argument between the actors. I was told that one of the performers, who played the father-in-law of the audience member-bride, had refused to act with the spectator allocated to him since that particular audience member happened to be his son. The actor was so adamant in his refusal to work with his son in the intimate spectatorship of *Cages* that another, significantly less-experienced actor, had to take on the role of the father-in-law. Clearly, this last-minute switch caused a lot of confusion behind the scenes, confusion that I was not privy to since I was sitting outside the house in which *Cages* was being staged. My own frustrations in the moment aside, what the matter ultimately boiled down to was that the cultural codes for this particular actor made it somehow impossible for him to engage in an intimate, interactive performance with his son. Was the actor's discomfort due to the fact that his son would be dressed as a woman and somehow, this would be 'demeaning'? Was it because the actor thought that he would intimidate his child, given the hierarchies present in their parent-child relationship? Whatever the reason, at the time at which this incident occurred, I chalked it up to one particular instance of one actor's idiosyncrasies. I especially thought this since we had other spectators in *Cages* with pre-existing relationships with some of the actors and the performances, in those other cases, proceeded without issue. However, when the question of knowing the actors resurged from actors and spectators in this very different context of the College, I was forced to revisit *Cages* and ask myself if that one encounter between father and son was actually symptomatic of a larger dilemma within the aesthetic of Immersive Theatre. What happens when there is a pre-existing relationship between spectators and actors in simulated, immersive environments? Especially in a conflict zone, when there are volatile political and personal histories in the mix, can a personal relationship between spectator and actor heighten the risk of an immersive piece?

In addition to such questions of identity, I am left with considerations about the kinds of empathy that might be evoked by different performance forms. If – as the data in this experiment indicates – using a form like Immersive Theatre could heighten emotion-based responses, does such an outcome become particularly ethically murky in contexts of conflict? Since anxiety levels are already high in a place of war, could heightened emotional responses veer toward the risky/dangerous end of the ethical spectrum? The spectators to *Cages* did not seem to indicate a particularly 'negative' experience in post-performance debriefs that we held. However, I do recall meeting one of the spectators a year after the performance when he said: "I still remember what you put me through that day." While this response is not necessarily problematic, in further thinking about the potential for immersive forms to heighten emotion-focused affects, I wonder if some of my disquiet lies in performances like *Fight or Flight* (2010), *Cages* (2013), *This Is Camp X-Ray* (UHC Collective, 2003), and *Chemins* (Haedicke, 2002) placing their spectators in the shoes of a *less* privileged Other, i.e., someone who is more oppressed, in the real world, than the audience member. Is it this relative positioning of powerlessness that increases anxiety within an aesthetic that also makes the spectator vulnerable with the demands made by its participatory/interactive quality? What if, instead, spectators were placed in more powerful positions of privilege? This is to say, instead of placing men in the shoes of women in *Cages*, what would have been the potential/limitations of placing women in the shoes of men – so that they could see how more privileged members of their communities negotiate power? But then again, haven't these approaches – of placing people in positions of power – been tried in the simulated environments of social psychology experiments like the Stanford Prison Experiment and Stanley Milgram's obedience experiments? Have such studies not shown us, time and time again, the dangers of giving people power over each other within the context of a simulated experience? While there are definitely risks associated with placing participants within an immersive/simulated experience, either in roles of complete power or complete powerlessness, is there a way for the theatre practitioner-researcher to find the space between these two extreme positions? And what might such a position be: between power and powerlessness, between prisoner and guard, between immigration official and asylum seeker? Would a shift in how we conceive characterization enable a more distanced empathy to occur even through a form like Immersive Theatre? Or is the important variable not the character that is given to spectator-participants but rather the notion of time? Was it the extended duration of the Stanford Prison Experiment that made the prisoner-participants abuse their positions of power whereas a shorter immersion in the role of the powerful, like in a one-hour performance of *Cages*, would address that issue? What is the place of time, then, in how various degrees of empathy and sympathy are evoked in a form like Immersive Theatre?

In addition to the persona that is given to the spectator-participant, characterization also links to what was identified by many spectators as the most interesting element for them in the Immersive Theatre piece – the character of the Fellow Detainee. An empathetic character that acts as a social referencing strategy, I postulate that the Fellow Detainee enabled audience member-participants to better understand the role that was given to them in the immersive performance. In contrast, *Cages* did not have any such sympathetic characters with which the audience member-bride could find a sense of comfort. While we had crafted the character of a brother who initially transitioned the spectator-participant into their role as a bride, the brother was also an agent who contributed to the bride's powerlessness in the marriage that was arranged for her. What if we had had introduced another character, of a woman – a mother-in-law, a sister-in-law – who would be a 'friendly' supporting character to take audience members through the immersive experience of *Cages*? While the character of the Fellow Detainee in this experiment emerged as the direct adaptation of a character from Kay Adshead's original text, could the intentional inclusion of a sympathetic character function as a way to address the discomfort induced by immersive forms, especially in contexts of conflict? The relevance of this kind of 'support', if I might call it that, can be seen in one of the conditions of the Milgram obedience experiments. As the reader might be aware, the most famous conclusion of these experiments was that when a volunteer-teacher was asked to administer electric shocks to an actor-student under the supervision of an actor-coordinator, 65 per cent of the teachers went up to the maximum of 450 volts (Perry, 2013:304). The lesser-known variations of this experiment, though, are when the volunteer-teachers were asked to administer shocks to an actor-student in the company of a group of fellow actor-teachers (roles that functioned as social referencing points) who either encouraged or dissuaded the volunteer-teacher from administering the shocks. When accompanied by these supporting actor-teachers, the results were quite different: 72 per cent of the volunteer-teachers administered 450 volts when encouraged by their fellow actor-teachers, while only 10 per cent of the volunteer-teachers administered the maximum 450 volts when dissuaded by fellow actor-teachers (Perry, 2013:305). This data suggests that the presence of a 'supporting' character has an impact on how spectator-participants engage with an immersive scenario – a strategy that could become useful in addressing some of the ethical questions that arise from the use of Immersive Theatre in any context, but specifically, in a place of conflict.

Another consideration that seems noteworthy is the contrast that emerged between the evocation of autobiographical memories in the immersive performance and the observation that, when looking across actors and spectators' data, there seemed to be more room for subjective interpretations in the immersive experience vis-à-vis real-world solutions for the problems in the piece. That said, it is evident how an evocation of autobiographical memories can become problematic in a context of war where such personal memories could be potentially traumatic – more so if conceptual processing means a later resurgence of these same memories. However, the reason I consider this particular outcome to be in contrast with the observation around subjectivity is that while the evocation of personal memories can be very problematic for the use of Immersive Theatre in a context of conflict, the potential for more subjectivity could be seen as a pedagogical outcome in contexts that are otherwise prone to black-and-white categorizations. And yet, an unconsidered/uncontrolled generation of autobiographical memories must give us cause for concern. Is there a way of bridging the gap between these possibilities? To thrive on the subjectivity afforded by Immersive Theatre but with the careful negotiation of autobiographical memories? I wonder if one strategy to address this question might lie in what I came to call 'process-based spectatorship' after my work on *Cages*. I initially considered this 'process-based spectatorship' in terms of using pre-performance workshops for spectators to address the extreme degrees of novelty in immersive forms. However, in light of the observations from this experiment, I wonder if invoking process-based spectatorship would be useful not only to address novelty but also to allow spectators the opportunity to create their own defence mechanisms upon knowing that the form could unleash autobiographical memories. Of course, the next question that emerges is *how* these concepts will be communicated to spectators in a way that both serves its purpose but also does not jeopardize the beauty of spontaneity within immersive aesthetics.

In addition to the aforementioned considerations, the emergence of the distinction between situational interest and topic interest is also a relevant discussion point. To remind the reader, as mentioned in Chapter 3, the kind of interest shown by spectators to the immersive experience was useful to consider as being situational when compared to the topic interest generated by the proscenium performance. Applying this potential difference to my work in Kashmir, would it be fair to say that through an experience like *Cages* – because of our chosen narrative around which to craft an immersive aesthetic – that audience members were far more intrigued by the situation that asked them to live in the shoes of a woman while she is a bride, rather than the application of this 'micro' issue to wider questions surrounding the links between gender and the conflicts in the region? I think back to one response from a spectator-participant to the piece who said, "I'm going to go back home and ask my wife how she felt on our wedding day" (ask her about a particular situation) as compared to a topical response like: "I'm going to go home and ask my wife how she feels about women's experiences in Kashmir." Immersing this spectator in the situation of a bride seemed to lead him to think precisely about that time in his life – interestingly parallel with the actors and spectators of the immersive piece in this experiment who seemed much more interested in individualized responses within scenarios, rather than in topics surrounding refugees and asylum seekers. At the same time, I recall that another spectator to *Cages* was far more interested in the topic of political violence that was alluded to in the piece and in this spectator's responses, he did not pay any attention to gender at all. So, clearly, applying the concept of situational interest to all immersive aesthetics might not be relevant outside the context of this project. However, what could be relevant is what a furthered understanding of different kinds of interest might tell us, as Applied Theatre researchers and practitioners. Do diverse forms of interest lead to varying real-world applications of knowledge? Or do distinctive forms of interest simply manifest in singular qualities of appreciation? Understanding the implications and manifestation of types of interest, therefore, does seem to warrant more extended investigation in uncovering the post-performance resonances of a piece of Immersive Theatre.

While all these considerations tend to be largely focused on the spectators' experiences in immersive experience, there are also a couple of considerations that I would like to highlight vis-à-vis performers' experiences in the two performances in this experiment. The first point that I would like to consider is my perception that the immersive piece's performers seemed far more excited about, and invested in, their work than their proscenium counterparts. I say 'perception' because of the significant difference in the numbers of performers in each piece and the fact that I had not designed specific tools to garner information about this specific dimension of the experiment. Given this perception, however, I consider the increased investment in the immersive performance to be due to the increased possibilities it contained for protagonism and due to the originality of the form for a novelty-seeking student body. In thinking about this (perception of) increased interest in the immersive performance's actors, I return to the experience of *Cages* and reflect on statements that were made to me by actors after that process. Having been previously exposed to only script-based, traditional forms of theatre making, the *Cages* actors spoke to finding excitement and new knowledge in making theatre in this (immersive) way. Interestingly this sentiment was much more muted among some of the older and more experienced actors, in particular, who expressed more resistance to the form. These actors did not seem to be comfortable with the lack of a structured script, and there was a palpable difference in how younger/less experienced and older/more experienced performers approached the immersive aesthetic. Placing this observation from *Cages* in conversation with my perception of actors' investment in this comparative experiment brings in an interesting question around actor demographics and how the prior training of a performer – within and outside a context of war – might have implications on the performers' engagement with immersive aesthetics.

The second point that I would like to highlight from the actors' feedback in this project is the notion of identification. Can the data in this experiment be interpreted to suggest that immersive actor training might necessitate a more holistic actor/character blend since performers have to be comfortable enough to improvise in response to unexpected audience contributions? And what are the implications of such a heightened actor-character blend in a context of war? Similar to the point made earlier about increased subjectivity among spectators to an immersive experience, could this point around character identification point toward an increased likelihood of subjectivity for actors as well? This potentially subjective actor/character blend includes the risk of actors changing the script within the privacy of their encounters – an occurrence that was seen in both *Cages* (the father-son occurrence) and in the experiment here (an instance that was mentioned earlier in this book). But does subjectivity also contain the pedagogical potential of enabling performers, especially in a conflict zone, to look beyond their own biases of good and bad, of black and white, of victim and perpetrator? For instance, if an actor who is a civilian has to portray someone from the army during an immersive experience, in having to find more identifiable links to the character that s/he is playing so as to be able to improvise in response to audience members' interactions, is there an increased likelihood of this actor trying to envision the Other? Whereas in script-based performances the actor might not need to work around personal biases to portray the Other, does a crossing over between Self/Other become more of a necessity with the demands of the immersive form?

With all these considerations in mind, the practitioner in me finds it only natural to subsequently wonder how each of these questions might be further explored in practice. Using the preceding reflections as a framing tool, therefore, I next use the concept of 'conditions' to propose future avenues of investigation, i.e., different conditions under which similar theatre lab experiments might need to be conducted in order to develop and further refine what emerged in this project. I borrow this particular approach of using conditions from an account of Milgram's obedience experiments (Perry, 2013) in which the twenty-four conditions under which the obedience experiment was conducted are listed alongside their particular results.[1] Using this framework in conversation with the deliberations earlier in this chapter, here are the conditions that I would like to explore in the future (in no specific order of importance).

Condition 1: Comparisons between immersive and proscenium theatre

The experiment described in this book, which involves the comparison between an immersive and proscenium piece about the same theme and invokes feedback from actors and spectators alike.

Condition 1a

Conducting a similar experiment but with increased numbers of spectators and the same number of performers in each piece, so as to confirm the suggestions that emerged in the data here. More numbers would be especially useful with regards to developing more nuanced insights into conceptual versus associative processing, defining and delineating the differences between situational and topic interest, and clarifying/categorizing the diverse kinds of empathy that might be evoked by each performance.

Condition 1b

Conducting a similar experiment that only focuses on the process of the actors. Through this process, explore the ways in which actors' ways of engaging with the material and their characters do/do not differ between immersive and proscenium performances.

Condition 1c

Conducting a similar experiment so as to investigate the similarities and differences between the ways amateur and more experienced actors engage with the two forms.

Condition 2: The actor/spectator relationship

To conduct the same immersive piece for two different audience groups: one group of spectators that has a personal relationship with the actors in the piece and the second group that does not. The purpose of this variation would be to gain more insights into whether or not a pre-existing relationship between actor and audience presents potential or challenges.

Condition 2a

Conducting a similar study as described in Condition 2, but with the added layer of looking at how the actor/spectator 'real-world' relationships impact how a proscenium piece is remembered. By comparing these outcomes with what emerges in Condition 2, could we begin to say which of these forms might more ethically function as an Applied Theatre aesthetic when audience members do/do not know their actors?

Condition 3: Time

What would it mean to design immersive experiences that deal with the same theme but last different lengths of time? What if one of the experiences immersed spectators for one hour while another immersed them in a similarly themed experience, but for twenty-four hours? The role of time in simulated experiences is something that has been highlighted before. Philip Zimbardo (2007:244), for example, says that his Stanford Prison Experiment "made it obvious that time perspective was not merely a personal trait or an outcome measure but could be altered by experiences in situations that expanded or contracted it."

Condition 3a

The condition above could also be applied toward comparing the function of time in differently durational proscenium performances. In so doing, could we glean some insights into whether or not Immersive Theatre shows distinguishably different outcomes than proscenium pieces when they both include a durational component – in comparison with the more subtle changes that evidenced themselves in this experiment, where both performances were of the same length?

Condition 4: Pre-performance workshops

Spectators in this experiment commented on the discomfort experienced during the immersive performance and also spoke of their desire to push the performance's limits and see what was possible. Furthermore, the evocation of autobiographical memories became a concern in the use of immersive environments as an Applied Theatre aesthetic. So, what would be the impact of framing an Immersive Theatre piece for spectators a day before the performance through the use of pre-performance sessions? Would audience members become better informed about the 'rules' of the world that they are about to enter and also be better prepared for the potentially visceral ways in which their memories might be evoked? This condition would involve comparing the experiences of a 'workshopped' spectator group to an immersive performance with the experiences of an audience group that does not have a pre-performance framing of the experience.

Condition 5: The other who is less oppressed

Intrigued by Zimbardo's (2007:450) question of whether we could use "the power [. . .] of the situation to produce virtue," I would like to consider the possibility of theatrical immersion that places the spectator in the shoes of someone who lies between 'oppressor' and 'oppressed' – not the 'helpless' inmate or the 'oppressive' guard, but other power positions that inhabit the space between all and no agency. How might the same immersive performance – one version in which spectators step into the shoes of the oppressed, one in which they are asked to participate as the oppressor, one in which they are asked to embody characters in the grey zone – lead to different effects?

Condition 6: The inclusion of a sympathetic character

Creating two immersive versions of the same piece: one in which the audience has a sympathetic accompanying character to take them through the immersive experience (like the Fellow Detainee); the other in which there is no such sympathetic character who accompanies the spectator-participant through the journey. Could this comparison give us more insight into the varying degrees of comfort/discomfort that might be experienced through the inclusion of an accompanying character that is played by an actor? I make the clarification that the sympathetic character is played by an actor since, in a simulation like the Stanford Prison Experiment, there were resonating characters to be found for each participant in other participant-prisoners. However, since all volunteer/spectator-participants are equally devoid of power in the structure of a simulated experiment, having an actor playing a sympathetic, accompanying role might have very different implications.

Condition 7: The implications of interest

Design a more nuanced data collection tool that assesses the different kinds of interest that might be generated by varying approaches to immersive aesthetics. While I remain unsure as to what such an experiment might actually look like – or if this might be a layer to add to one or more of the these conditions rather than being explored in isolation – the notion of interest does seem to be worthy of more investigation.

The aforementioned list of conditions is not exhaustive, of course, and more thought needs to be given to which condition might need to be tested before or after another. Like much practice-based research I expect this list of conditions to be in a continual state of evolution, and by including them here, I hope that they will serve as prompts for other theatre practitioner-researchers who share my interest in better understanding what Immersive Theatre 'does'.

A final memo from my theatre lab

One month seemed a long time for some of the participants in this research project to record journal entries and to keep track of the ways in which they recalled their performances. Many of the actors and spectators said that the process was not necessarily convenient and was almost doomed to 'fail' given the many other time commitments that each of them had as part of their schedules at the College. And yet, as I conclude this experiment, I find myself wondering about other mechanisms and strategies that might have been designed so as to garner longer-term insights into how spectators react to, and remember, specific aesthetic forms. Clearly the availability of, and possibility for, this kind of longitudinal data is problematic in qualitative research. And yet, this is one of the questions that I find myself left with. Since it is the most unpredictable of situations that often lead us to recall a book that we have read or a film that we have watched, months or even years later, can a one-month study even come close to exploring what a performance actually 'does' for its performers or spectators?

And furthermore, what are the implications of generating theory from a small sample size as in this project when seeking to create larger understandings about a form of theatre? Did I generate 'enough' data in this project to be able to justify the ideas that I have proposed? Although I agree with the spirit of the method of instances that was mentioned earlier in this book, in that even one interview could be enough basis from which to craft context-specific analyses of a particular situation, this 'micro' approach certainly does not have the spectacular quality of decisive results that are produced by other experiments that test simulated environments.

As I ask myself these questions though, and as I continue to ruminate upon the limitations of the data that this project generated, I have to keep reminding myself that experiments such as these are not about looking for universal theories, but rather about engendering new lenses through which to view existing concerns.

That experiments like these do not seek to reach decisions about the effect of one form over another, but rather, they aim to generate different queries and/or ask the same queries differently.

That, ultimately, experiments like these (at least, for me) are about catalyzing new questions, or better-informed old questions; questions that I will take with me into the next stage of experiments in my theatre lab.

Note

1 1. No feedback
    This variation tests how an almost silent learner may affect obedience. The learner, in the adjoining room, does not cry out. Nothing is heard from him until the twentieth shock (300 volts), when he pounds on the wall. He pounds again at 315 volts, and then is silent.
    Number of subjects: 40
    Number who went to 450 volts: 65 percent
    2. Voice feedback
    Perhaps the best-known variation, this tests the effect of a vocal learner as the teacher hears his cries and shouts from the adjoining room. The first sound from the learner is a grunt at the fifth shock (75 volts). At the tenth shock (150 volts), he demands to be let out. His protests and cries increase in intensity with each subsequent shock.
    Number of subjects: 40
    Number who went to 450 volts: 62 percent
    [The list continues as such with twenty-four different conditions under which Milgram's premise was tested].

Works cited

Cages. 2013. Performance. Srinagar, Kashmir.
Fight or Flight. 2010. Performance. Pune, India.
Haedicke, S. C. 2002. The politics of participation: *Un Voyage Pas Comme Les Autres Sur Les Chemins De L'Exil. Theatre Topics.* 12(2):99–118.
Perry, G. 2013. *Behind the Shock Machine: The Untold Story of the Notorious Milgram Psychology Experiments.* New York and London: New Press.
UHC Collective. 2003. *This Is Camp X-Ray.* Performance. Manchester, UK.
Zimbardo, P. 2007. *The Lucifer Effect: Understanding How Good People Turn Evil.* New York: Random House.

Index

Printed in the United States
by Baker & Taylor Publisher Services